# DOMESTIC POLITICS AND FOREIGN POLICY
## Perspectives on India-Pakistan Relations

# DOMESTIC POLITICS AND FOREIGN POLICY

## Perspectives on India-Pakistan Relations

*Sanjeev Kumar H.M.*

UPPAL PUBLISHING HOUSE
NEW DELHI - 110002 (India)

**UPPAL PUBLISHING HOUSE**
3 Ansari Road, Darya Ganj, New Delhi - 110002
Phones: 23273756, 23286571, Fax: 91-011-23286571
Email: uppalbooks@vsnl.net


First Published 2007
ISBN: 978-81-7658-041-0
010: 81-7658-041-4



**Printed in India**

Published by B.S. Uppal for Uppal Publishing House, 3 Ansari Road, Darya Ganj, New Delhi and Typeset by Priyanka Graphics, Laxmi Nagar, Delhi and Printed at Arora Offset Press, Delhi-110092..

# Preface

The nature of India's foreign policy has not only been conditioned by external sources. But the dominant presence of various domestic factors in the process of its evolution and enactment has been crucial. When India emerged as a liberal democracy after attaining independence, political parties assumed a predominant role in policy processes by acting as a vital domestic element of the polity. Through their perception of major international developments and by rendering policy prescriptions, they have demonstrated their meaningful presence in the foreign policy making process.

The nettled relations with Pakistan which has emerged as a major challenge confronted by independent India, has figured as one of the predominant external factors that has significantly influenced the nature and direction of India's foreign policy. British India was divided in a haste, with many prevalent socio-political problems left unaddressed. The intensity of these problems rather than being reduced got re-doubled after partition, leading to inscribing of deep scars in their bilateral relations.

As a result, mistrust and animosity have been the premier characters of the politics of the sub-continent that has been demonstrated by four wars and several ineffective agreements. This has compelled India's foreign policy makers to be enmeshed in one single issue, that is management of the country's relations with Pakistan. This phenomenon has governed significant stages in the evolution of India's foreign policy.

In this work an endeavour has been made to understand the perception of political parties towards vital issues in India Pakistan relations. On the basis of the approach of political parties and their policy prescriptions, the nature of India's foreign policy towards Pakistan has been examined. This work does not claim to make a detailed analysis of the evolution, the procedural aspect and overall dynamics of India's foreign policy. But it seeks to understand the interface between the approach of political parties and foreign policy making process in India, specifically the policies apropos Pakistan.

To explain this inter-connection, two principle issues that have largely occupied the landscape of India's foreign policy have been examined. Firstly, the Kashmir issue that has engrossed the overall dynamics of India-Pakistan relations, has been identified as a serious foreign policy challenge. It has remained as a cliff-hanger for over six decades.

Some structural factors of the two countries symbolising their nationalistic agendas, pressed them to a conflict over the territory of Jammu&Kashmir. To be precise, India's abstinence to hold on to Jammu&Kashmir to exhibit its secular credentials and Pakistan's irredentism reflecting its paranoiac urge to justify its stance on the two-nation theory have kept the two countries locked in a constant state of conflict.

The second prominent issue has been the overt acquisition of nuclear weapons by both the countries and its ramifications for their bilateral relations. This phenomenon has also brought a critical dimension to the exasperated Kashmir issue. The presence of a nuclear capable Pakistan in the region, has totally engaged the thoughts and actions of the foreign policy establishment in India and it cannot remain oblivious of this changed politico-strategic environment. In accordance to this the country's foreign policy has to be readjusted and provided a new vigour to deal with these fresh and serious challenges.

These two issues have coupled together and considerably fashioned the contemporary India-Pakistan relations. Hence in this work I have attempted to analyse the perception of political parties towards India-Pakistan relations from the perspective of these two issues and their policy recommendations to deal with them. This largely facilitates the comprehension of the nature and different dimensions of India's foreign policy towards Pakistan.

Although number of works already exist in the field concerning the inter-face between domestic politics and foreign policy. But none of them have made a comprehensive examination of how far the perception and policy responses of political parties have influenced the nature of India's foreign policy towards Pakistan. I have tried to plug this lacuna by examining the role of political parties in the shaping of India's policy responses to the major issues in which India-Pakistan relations are convoluted.

Besides, the recent trends in India's foreign policy that have occurred after the changed politico-strategic environment of the region, engendered due to the overt nuclear weaponisation of the two sub-continental neighbours. Entails a wider comprehension of the domestic influences on the shaping of India's foreign policy towards Pakistan. The primary reason for this is that the Indian nuclear weapons program is rooted in the civilian nuclear research that involves greater civilian control. Thus marking a preeminent role for political parties in the process of the formulation of nuclear policy, be it civilian or military.

Above all, globalization of national economies characterized by the circumventing of national borders has led to increased linkages between domestic and international environments. The present Indian foreign policy has to be understood from the perspective of these dynamics. This task can be accomplished in a dexterous manner by an examination of the perception of political parties on major issues of international politics. Their evaluation of the prevailing international situation and their policy suggestions will provide deeper insights into the nature of India's policy towards crucial issues such as those concerning India-Pakistan relations.

**Sanjeev Kumar, H.M.**

# Acknowledgements

I wish to express deep sense of gratitude to various individuals and organizations without whose help and assistance this work would not have been accomplished. My Research Guide, Dr. S.S.Patagundi, Professor Department of Political Science, Karnatak University, Dharwad Karnataka, should head this list. His able and keen supervision, constant encouragement and generous help enabled me to sail through the difficult phases during the completion of this work. Any adept articulations present in this book are the result of his guidance and all short comings are mine. I also sincerely acknowledge the help of Dr. Rajpal Budania, Sandeep Pankaj and Alok Prasad my colleagues at University of Allahabad, whose continued support and constructive criticism benefited the refinement of this work.

I was fortunate to receive valuable insights on various issues discussed in this book by interacting with many individuals. In this regard I would like to extend my gratitude to Dr. K. Raghavendra Rao, Professor, University of Mangalore, Prof. Rajendra Govind Harshe, Vice Chancellor University of Allahabad, Prof. Kalim Bahadur, Dr. Uma Singh, and Dr. Rakesh Gupta, Faculty Members, Jawaharlal Nehru University, New Delhi, P.S. Jayaramu, Professor of Political Science Bangalore University, C. Rajamohan, strategic Analyst and Mr. Muchkund Dube former foreign secretary, Government of India.

It is my duty to thankfully acknowledge the assistance and co-operation of the staff members of the following libraries: (i) Karnatak University Library, Dharwad, (ii) Jawaharlal Nehru University Library, New Delhi, (iii) Indian Council of World Affairs Library, New Delhi, (iv) Delhi University Library, New Delhi, (v) Indian Council of Social Science Research Library, New Delhi, Indo-American center for International Studies, Hyderabad and Hyderabad central university Library, Hyderabad.

My thanks are also due to my friends and well wishers- Mr. Maneesh Pandey, Dr. Alakananda Shringare, Krishna Hombal, N. Ramesh Reddy, Subhash Patil and Arvind K. for their co-operation in one way or the other that facilitated the speedy completion of this work. Last but not the least, I would like to express my heartiest thanks to my beloved wife Pushpa, who has been a fountain of inspiration and harbinger of courage and strength who constantly supported me throughout the completion of this work.

**Sanjeev Kumar, H.M.**

# Contents

# Chapter 1

# Introduction

Democratisation of national and international affairs has meant that both domestic and international politics have been engrossed by one single phenomenon that is democracy. It has gained wider currency and acknowledgement in the epoch of globalisation and has emerged as a universal standard that determines the virtue of political action, both in the internal and external spheres of a polity. Now, democracy is not just a matter of semantics, indicative of a form of Government, but it has attained the recognition of a doctrine, regulating a spectrum of human activities.

The modern liberal democracy has graduated to the present form, under the influence of myriad of factors. But the impact of the existence of a sound and stable system of political parties has been decisive. They not only have contributed significantly in activating the political system, but also provide an institutional character to the prevalent public opinion in the polity.

People's participation is essential for democratizing policy making process. But since modern States are large nation-states, direct people's participation is inconceivable. Hence the role of political parties assumes a momentous character. They are the custodians of public interest and perform the task of mobilising public opinion and act as instruments of interest articulation and interest aggregation. On the whole, political parties are a link between the citizens and Government. They discuss various issues pertaining to public interest in the parliament and express the people's will and aspirations and contribute to the formulation of a sound domestic and foreign policy. "In the course of the analysis, two functions, or two major systemic roles of parties, have come to the fore: expression and channelment. A third function, communication, needs to be entered for the completeness of the argument."[1]

A country regulates its international affairs, through a prudent foreign policy. In order to rationally deal with political, economic, social and cultural issues in the ambit of the country's external affairs, foreign policy of a country should be well equipped and adaptable to the turbulence of world politics and calibrated to adjust to the domestic tumult. In other words, foreign policy is deeply influenced by domestic milieu which in turn is influenced by the prevailing international situation. Thus, foreign policy makers must take proper cognizance of the interface between domestic politics and foreign affairs of a State, while molding its foreign policy.

In a democracy, the responsibility of formulating a sagacious foreign policy lies primarily with political parties; as they form the institutional structures that opperatise the polity and forms its bedrock. Foreign policy response of a nation considerably rests upon the approach of political parties towards various issues concerning the country's external affairs. Their perception of international situation and articulation of domestic public opinion act as qualitative inputs for molding a rational foreign policy. If there are any lapses and loop holes in the enactment and execution of foreign policy, the reactions of the political parties to these inconsistencies forms a formidable feedback for bringing reforms to the existing policies.

If the number of neighbours juxtaposed to a country is on the higher side, then it adverts for greater caution while evolving its foreign policy which should be rational enough to minimize bellicosity and maximize co-operation. "Relations and policy towards neighbours is of paramount importance for any country. All countries want peace and security on their borders and friendly neighbours to live with. Not many have managed to succeed as history and traditions, no less than size and resources, have often accentuated divergences and conflicts among neighbouring countries. But the priority and primacy of place that they occupy in a country's foreign relations cannot be doubted. This has been equally true of India."[2]

Pakistan has factored significantly in the foreign policy agenda of India and it has occupied the perception of political parties as the most vital question confronting defence strategists and foreign policy makers. This has been due to the unending adversarial relations between the two that sprung immediately after partition. "The partition of the sub-continent after centuries of organic existence, far from ending the rivalry, intensified it. The problems arising out of partition and the problems of neighbourhood between the two countries with memories of the communal holocaust immediately preceding the partition further enhanced this rivalry."[3]

The dismantling of colonial manacles in the sub-continent was followed by the emergence of a political strife, which divided the region into two hostile and ideologically divergent nations; India and Pakistan. This was supervened by a pathetic course of bitter bilateral relations between the two. The history of Indo-Pakistan relations over the years has been a chronicle of four wars and several ineffective agreements. On the whole, the entire gamut of Indo-Pakistan relations has been influenced by contentious issues causing tension between the two countries. Overall, conflict has been the fundamental character of India Pakistan relations.

The foreign policies of the Government of India and Pakistan accord top priority to the issues involved in their bilateral relations. The blemished texture of their relations has been a subject of immense interest for scholars, politicians and the media in both the countries. In India the major national parties while in power or in opposition have made scrupulous attempts to find amicable solutions to this protracted dispute. But they have been futile and the desired results still appear to be fictitious. Hence an examination of the relations between India and Pakistan has become a constant requirement.

Political parties, as institutional mechanisms of Indian political system, have contributed significantly in dealing with Indo-Pakistan relations. In this context, how political parties perceive the problems of Indo-Pakistan relations determines the effectiveness of India in identifying remedial measures. In view of this, an attempt has been made in this study to examine the problems of Indo-Pakistan relations from the perspective of India's major national parties such as the Indian National Congress, Bhartiya Janta Party, Janta Party, Janata Dal and the two main left parties, CPI and the CPI [M]

To accomplish this task, two issues that have over determined all other considerations in deciding the contemporary fabric of India Pakistan relations, have been identified. They are: (1) the Kashmir issue (2) the issue of nuclear weaponisation. They have a major bearing on foreign policy and defence strategies of both the countries. The unsatisfactory process of partition led to the emergence of protracted tension between India and Pakistan over the issue of Kashmir. Both countries advance vociferous claims over the territory of Kashmir. Their geo-political interests depend upon their control over Kashmir. The region's strategic importance for both has been illustrated by Sisir Gupta. He indicates: "for India Kashmir is Vital for the security of the country as a whole in the face of growing military pressures from the north and the threat of a co-ordinated military adventure by two hostile neighbours. For Pakistan the stakes were equally weighty. The relative status of India and Pakistan would be changed in Pakistan's favour, if she were to secure Kashmir."[4]

The deadlock over Kashmir resulted in the ignition of proxy war, contrived in the name of religion by Pakistan through its cabal consisting of the ISI, by fostering militant outfits to spread terror. This ultimately had serious implications on Indo-Pakistan relations and terrorism has become a premier source of tension between the two. The gravity of the issue has been spelt out thus: "Pakistan's sponsored cross-border terrorism since 1980's 'in flagrant violation of international delegations"[5], "first in Punjab and since 1988 in Kashmir has remained the most disturbing and dangerous phenomenon drawing serious regional and global attention. While proper co-ordination and the commitment of State and its police plus maximum public co-operation controlled insurgency in Punjab, in the case of Kashmir it has taken recourse to proxy war and therefore, it persists."[6]

Another important antecedent that has brought a perilous dimension to India Pakistan relations is the declared nuclear weapons status of both the countries. After India and Pakistan gained potential nuclear weapons capability, threats to the security and stability of the entire South Asian region has been inflated. It is considered: "Until India and Pakistan successfully embedded their nuclear weapons in robust command, control, communications and intelligence infrastructure, the risk of inadvertent or, worse, unauthorized usage will persist."[7] "Ironically, American non-proliferation policy, in its single minded zeal to prevent the proliferation of nuclear weapons, also prohibits the transfer of certain technologies that might mitigate the dangers of accidental nuclear war."[8]

Hence a precise understanding of Indian policy response to these challenges needs a comprehensive examination of the perception and attitude of the major Indian political parties towards these trenchant policy issues. Being the part of Government and also representing the citizens in the parliament, they form a vital link between the Government and the public. Hence their crucial role in identifying policy options cannot be undermined.

## *Reference*

1. Giovanni, Sartori, *Parties and Party System: A Framework for Analysis*, Vol. I, Cambridge University Press, London, 1976, p. 4.

2. V.P., Dutta, *India's Foreign Policy*, Vikas Publishing House, New Delhi, 1984, p. 136.

3. Aswini, K. Ray, *Domestic Compulsions and Foreign Policy, Pakistan in Indo-Soviet Relations 1947-1958,* Manas Publications, New Delhi, 1975, p. 1.

4. Sisir Gupta, *Kashmir: A Study in Indo-Pakistan Relations,* Asia Publishing House, Bombay, 1966, pp. 442-43.

5. Aziz Ahmed, *Islamic Culture in Indian Environment,* Oxford University Press, Delhi, 1999, p. 214.

6. C. K., Choudhary, Cross-Border Terrorism : Pakistan's Compulsions, *Constraints and Stakes, India Quarterly,* 57(2), April-June, 2001, p. 40.

7. Shaun Gregory, A Formidable Challenge : Nuclear Command and Control in South Asia, *Disarmament Diplomacy,* No. 54, February 2001, pp. 2-4.

8. Ashley Tellis, India's Emerging Nuclear Posture, cited in Sumit Ganguly, *Conflict Unending, India-Pakistan Tensions Since 1947,* Oxford University Press, New Delhi, 2002, p.109

Chapter 2

# Domestic Politics and International Relations

"There is an integral relationship between domestic politics and foreign affairs of a country."[1] The convergence of the two is inevitable for all modern political systems. The genteel conduct of affairs in both spheres depends upon the pattern of their interactions. A healthy interface between them facilitates the maintenance of equilibrium in the system. The confluence of the domestic environment and the international milieu will determine the nature and content of policies formulated by a country to deal with the affairs at home and abroad.

The capability of a country to counter global challenges largely depends on its domestic strength. "A country, which faces turmoil in domestic politics, cannot withstand the turbulence of world politics."[2] Hence lack of proper liaison between the two spheres may disturb the equilibrium of a system, resulting in its destabilisation.

The domestic strength of a country presupposes the existence of a sound economy, stable polity, strong military, sound socio-political institutions and a vibrant civil society. The position of a country in the realm of world affairs will mainly rest upon the constructive role played by these variables within the polity. Domestic imbalances may lead to the disturbance of international relations. The turmoil in Baluchistan which was purely an internal matter of Pakistan, was disturbed its external affairs that is, it was affected to a considerable extent the peace process between India and Pakistan.

On the other hand, the domestic space of a country is not sequestered from the influence of the factors active beyond its territorial limits. The changing international situations affected by strong global forces have deep-rooted repercussions on the internal affairs of a country. The external variables such as international organizations, big power politics, international economic order, major international crises and relations with neighbours, considerably influence domestic space of a polity. The publication of Prophet Mohammad's caricatures thousands of miles away provoked discontentment among the Muslims in India leading to minor communal squabbles. This symbolises a globalisation syndrome, where there are soft borders and a time-space compression. Thus the interlocking balances between domestic space and the international environment cannot be undermined.

The stakes of a nation in world politics is to a large extent determined by the nature of its foreign policy. But it is not merely influenced by the prevailing international situation; the impact of domestic politics is also definitive. Hence, "Foreign policy of a country is the projection of domestic policy, the policy makers are linked with the internal and international environment. Foreign policy and domestic politics have become increasingly inter-related."[3]

The inter-connection between domestic and international politics has snow balled in recent times. The globalisation of national economies and the subsequent retreat of the State endorse our observation. The distances and barriers between the countries have been circumvented. According to Stanley Hoffmann : "The dichotomy between international and domestic politics is getting eroded."[4] This interface has got crystallized after the end of cold war. Adam Przeworski, noted: "Global structural changes in the post cold war era would certainly affect the functioning of the domestic political system."[5]

Foreign policy is an instrument by which a country manages its international affairs and it reflects its national interest. The nature of a country's foreign policy determines its role in international arena. weakness of foreign policy, negates its role in global affairs. Hence, foreign policy is a set of principles and objectives formulated by a country aiming at harmonising its interests with that of the fellow members in the family of nations. Modelski viewed : "The foreign policy problem is essentially a question of adjusting the actions of States to each other."[6]

A country's foreign policy does not operate in a vacuum. It functions in a matrix of internal and external forces. In this study foreign policy has been considered as a dependent variable which is influenced by several independent variables stemming out both from the domestic environment of the polity and the international milieu surrounding it. The integral connectivity between domestic and international environments forms one of the primary determinants of the nature of a country's foreign policy.

Domestic compulsions profoundly influence the foreign policy making process of Foreign policy makers by and large must act in accordance to the demands of diverse groups in the internal sphere. As these groups view the international environment from the prism of their own perceptions, an arduous task for the foreign policy makers is to synchronize these diametrical viewpoints in order to provide a consensual character to the country's foreign policy. Mayer Frederick has observed: "When nations negotiate often the toughest bargaining is not among nations but within them. Experienced negotiators almost invariably insist that the more difficult part of their job does not consist in dealing with their adversaries across the table. But in handling interest groups, bureaucrats and politicians at home."[7]

Similarly, the prevailing international situation has a substantial impact upon the foreign policy making process. For instance the ongoing American war against terrorism has been a vital factor in India's moderation of its intransigent policy of non-alignment and making a historic policy shift in concluding the July 18th deal for civilian nuclear co-operation with the United States. The motivational compulsions that have driven India to make such drastic policy shift seems to be India's urge to receive American cooperation in countering cross-border terrorism perpetrated against it. National interest being the permanent guide for foreign policy makers, India's genuine security concerns has factored into a fundamental transformation of the nation's foreign policy.

Ultimately, domestic politics and foreign policy cannot be understood in isolation. Their inter-locking balances are crucial to determine the nature of each one of them. For a broader understanding of the nature of foreign policies from the viewpoint of diverse political systems, it is felicitous to understand the complex interaction between the domestic environment and the foreign policy making process in a political system. The domestic environment comprises several variables which play a momentous role in shaping the foreign policy of a country. Political parties are one of the most significant institutional variables which have a dominant role in the process of moulding a country's foreign policy in a democracy.

Political system which is regarded as the sub-system of international system comprises several components. Political parties which constitute a party system are recognized as one of the most important sub-systems of a political system. The popular character of political parties renders to them a crucial position in the political system and their role in policy processes is decisive. James N. Rosenau has provided a theoretical framework to explain the definitive impact of domestic politics on foreign policy, thus: "In order to facilitate the development of linkage theory, we now expand the foregoing into a larger framework in which twenty four aspects of politics that might serve or give rise to outputs and inputs have been identified. Along with six aspects or [from the polity perspective] sub-environment of the international system that might generate or receive outputs and inputs."[8]

The process of democratization facilitated the emergence of political parties as key structures of a political system and their scope and importance has rapidly grown in spite of the fact that they are extra-constitutional entities. The political processes in a liberal democracy are propelled and conditioned by political parties. They constitute an important component of the structural mechanism involved in enacting a country's foreign policy. But it is lamentable that the field of foreign policy studies, dealing with the interface between political parties and foreign policy, has been suffering from impoverishment, because of the lack of contribution from the scholars of foreign policy to analyse the complex and inevitable interaction between political parties and foreign policy. Marcel Merle observes: "Political science and international relations have become separated by a gulf into which the question of the connection between political parties and foreign policy seems to have fallen into oblivion."[9]

The mass support base that political parties commend in a democracy, enables them to exert more influence on the process of policy enactment than any other institution. To such an extent that even the responsiveness of a political system is largely determined by the capability of its party system. Further, its effectiveness in countering internal and global challenges depends to a considerable extent upon the existence of a healthy party system.

Hence, political parties are an indispensable element of a democracy. The growing significance of political parties for democracy has led some scholars to describe democracy as partycracy. Political parties reflect man's nature of sociability. The sociability of individuals prompts them to involve themselves in different groups and they take crucial decisions after discussion. In this regard party politics is an important activity in a democratic polity depicting man as a social animal. Hence, the nature of his socio-economic and political life in a democracy is to a great deal molded by their involvement in the activities of political parties.

Citizens' participation in policy processes through their indulgence in the course of discussions relating to premier policy issues is a fundamental prerequisite of a democracy. But the geo-physical limitations of modern nation States and their societal complexities obliterate the feasibility of direct participation of all citizens. Political parties, as organized structures of a political system, act as a bridge between the citizens and the Government and on behalf of the citizens, they take part in the process of settling major policy matters. In this way they democratise the policy processes by their active engagement.

There are various methods of analysing the nexus between domestic politics and foreign affairs of a democratic political system. Conceivably one of the most expedient ways to comprehend this interconnection is by studying the role of political parties in the process of formulation of foreign policy. Since political parties are a fundamental component of the political process of a polity, they have a greater leverage in determining the foreign policy position of every polity. The stance of political parties over foreign policy issues greatly depends upon their perception, and the same is fashioned by the domestic and international milieu. The changing domestic scenario and the dynamics of international situation have a major bearing on the attitude of political parties towards foreign policy issues.

Discrepancy in the perception of different political parties regarding domestic and international environment is obvious. This divergence is primarily molded by the ideology and principles underpinning a particular party. This results in the emergence of differences among political parties on policy alternatives. Apart from this, the parliamentary position of political parties has a major impact on its role in the foreign policy making process.

Foreign policy makers are influenced by the way in which political parties perceive international situations, policy options and the consequence of various policy alternatives. The reactions of political parties to various policies executed act as a feedback to policy makers. On the other hand, political parties including the ruling party, formulate broad policy guidelines on the basis of their ideology, principles, programmes and electoral promises.

As Governments in a democracy are party Governments, the policy makers are inextricably linked up with the ruling party and there is a conspicuous impact of its ideology, principles and programmes on the people concerned with the enactment of foreign policy. The policy makers also come under the impact of opposition parties while formulating their foreign policy. The opposition parties contribute to the process by their constant engagement in debates and discussions of various issues of foreign policy. The members of the Government are in a direct interaction with the opposition parties on the floor of parliament.

Their comments and criticisms on any foreign policy initiative of the Government and the questions on acute issues will influence the foreign policy makers. Above all, the ruling and opposition parties are at mutual interaction, when the ruling party consults all other parties for bringing a consensus on a critical foreign policy matter. Political parties apprise the Government regarding the impact of a proposed policy. On the whole, the political parties influence the foreign policy makers by their evaluation of the international situation, suggestion of policy alternatives and advice on the framework for execution of foreign policy. In this way, foreign policy objectives and the needs of people are correlated.

Foreign policy must be devised in such a manner that it should boost the potency of a political system to fulfill people's needs. Due to time constraints, foreign policy makers may not be able to go down to the grass root levels to comprehend people's interests. Political parties bridge the gap between the Government and public. They perform the task of interest articulation and interest aggregation and enlighten the policy makers about the needs of people. This integral connection between the political parties and foreign policy makers denotes the pertinence of the study of the role of political parties in the process of foreign policy formulation. George Modelski indicates: "Political partys' importance for the study of foreign policy lies in the fact that they are generally speaking nation-wide in scope and reflect a variety of interests."[10]

The influential role of political parties in modern political systems includes their decisive participation in foreign policy making process. Thus a correlation of the attitude of political parties and foreign policy making process is inevitable. Research in this area is important because of the dynamic nature of the subject. The reason for this is the oscillation in the policy position of political parties. They change their policy stance periodically owing to the impact of changes in domestic and international milieu, which counsel for an unstinted examination of the dynamics of the field. Summing up the significant role played by the political parties in the process of foreign policy formulation, Marcel Merle viewed: "The role played by the political parties in the formulation of foreign policy should be a particularly active one. By virtue of their relations on the one hand with those in power and on the other hand with public opinion, the parties find themselves at the crossroads of the interaction between them and the external affairs."[11]

## *References*


1. Navnita Chadha, Behera, India-Pakistan Relations : Alternative Foreign Policy Options, in Lalit Mansingh ed., *India's Foreign Policy Agenda for the 21st Century,* Vol. 2, Konark Publishers, New Delhi, 1997, p.236.

2. S.S., Patagundi *Urban Elites Perception of India's Foreign Policy,* Research Report submitted to the Indian Council of Social Science Research, New Delhi, 1993, p. 12.

3. Stanely, Hoffmann, ed, *Contemporary Theory in International Relations,* Prentice Hall of India, New Delhi, 1964, p. 4.

4. Stanely Hoffmann's remarks in a conference on *US Foreign Policy : 1988-1994,* held on 21-22 April 1995 at the Centre for International Affairs, Howard University, Cambridge, Massachusetts, 1995, p. 5.

5. Adam Przeworski, quoted in James N. Rosenau, *Turbulence in World Politics : A Theory of Change and Continuity*, Princeton University Press, Princeton, 1990, p. 22.

6. George, Modelski, *A Theory of Foreign Policy,* Pallmall, London, 1962, pp. 3-4.

7. Mayer Frederick, Managing domestic differences in international negotiations: the strategic use of internal side-payments, *International organization,* 46[4] Autum, 1992, p.793.

8. Marcel Merle, *Political parties and Foreign Policy in Pluralist Regimes, International Social Science Journal,* 30 (1), 1978, pp.73-74.

9. James N. Rosenau, towards the study of national international linkages, in James N. Rosenau ed, *Linkage politics*, the free press, New York, 1969, p.49.

10. George, Modelski, Supra, No. 6, p. 74.

11. Marcel Merle, Supra, No. 7, pp.75-76.

# Chapter 3

# Partition of the Indian Sub-Continent

The unprecedented catastrophe that marked the division of the sub-continent engendered such an intractable animosity between the two divided nations India and Pakistan that the resolution of their disputes seems to be a pipe dream. The ever existent conflictual nature of their bilateral relations, owes its origin to a considerable extent, to that dark epoch in South Asian history. The lamentable partition of the subcontinent was an outcome of a perennial ripening of repugnance between Hindus and Muslims and it was not an abrupt event.

Though both the communities lived together as a fraternity imbibing a composite culture, the ambivalent religio-cultural ethos and the deleterious political forces that operated at the time of British imperial regime perturbed the existing harmonious relations between the two communities.

These two antecedents acted as catalysts for accretion of differences between the two communities. "Their hostilities originated in the long period of Muslim rule over India, which lasted nearly a thousand years before the advent of European colonial powers."[1] But even after this, the Indian society was able to sustain its properties as a multi-cultural and pluralistic society, until the British colonial rule was established.

"Before the arrival of the British in India, Hindus and Muslims lived in peace with each other. Maybe, in somewhat, specified social compartments, quite akin to the customs yet, accommodating each other's religious beliefs."[2] When the British took over the centre stage of Indian society, it was divided on communal lines. They fashioned their policies on the basis of the principle of divide and rule. The first expression of which, can be seen when Lord Curzon divided the province of Bengal. This went a long way in determining the future status of the Indian subcontinent.

Besides this, the British introduced the system of a separate electorate and reservation of seats in the popular assembly on the basis of communal lines. This sinister move crystallised the mutual antagonism between the two communities and led to cultural altercations of unimaginable proportions, ultimately leading to the geo-political separation of people who had imbibed a composite culture.

Further, regarding the conflict between India and Pakistan, which has pronounced ligature with the rueful events leading to partition of Indian sub-continent. "Some have suggested that the conflict has a primordial basis and is rooted in the divergent and essentially antithetical world views of Islam and Hinduism."[3] This antipathy is deeply entrenched in the turbulent times of the British rule in India.

At the outset, when the British introduced western education, only a few progressive Hindus came forward to relish the opportunity. Muslims were obstinate because they nurtured abhorrence towards the British and were obsessed by the notion that they had wrested India's reigns of power from them. This led to their inhibition towards western education and they desisted from participating in the mainstream socio-political affairs under the British regime.

On the other hand, the Hindus accepted western education and got opportunities to participate in the lower strata of British administration. Their socio-economic status witnessed a phenomenal uplift. British also preferred the progressive and liberal Hindus rather than the orthodox and conservative Muslims. All this widened the rift between the two communities.

At this juncture some of the Muslim elites felt that their community was lagging behind in comparison to Hindus. The need was to accept the challenges of the hour and modernise through the means of western education. The forerunner of this idea was Sir Syed Ahamed Khan, who sniffed a threat to Muslim identity. He urged them to modernise by embracing western education. Sir Syed's aim seemed to make Muslims more Islam-conscious rather than broad- minded secularists.

This appears to be the first heedful step towards Muslim separatism and a bid to arouse a sense of unity among them and to preserve the identity of their culture. Sir Siyeed became instrumental in the inception of several organisations prominent among them being Mohamadan Anglo Oriental College, which is known today as Aligarh Muslim University. This institution became the hub of Muslim resuscitation. Sir Siyed was the first Muslim intellectual to express the threats of the ghost of Hindu Raj. That is the political domination of Hindus if India was to be freed from the colonial yoke. This conviction engraved the seeds of Muslim separatism, which propelled them to demand a separate geo-political status, distinct from that of Hindus.

Former Prime Minister of Pakistan Liaquat Ali Khan, articulated: "Pakistan came into being as a result of the urge felt by the Muslims of the sub-continent to secure a territory. However limited, where Islamic ideology and way of life could be practiced and demonstrated to the World."[4]

The formation of Muslim League, was a benchmark in the string of events leading to India's partition. In the course of events, the League became a platform for Muslim leaders to articulate their claims and it became the cornerstone of the movement for the creation of Pakistan.

## Two Nation Theory

India's partition can be traced to the "historical logic of the two-nation theory"[5], which formed the primary source of friction between Hindus and Muslims. The roots of separatism can be found in the jarring ideological predilections of Hindus and Muslims. Their proclivities were embodied in the vituperative framework of "The two-nation theory which became a dividing line of India's partition and continues to be a principal source of conflict between Pakistan's Islamic ideology and India's secular nationalism."[6]

The two-nation theory states that Hindus and Muslims are two different nations and require two different geographical entities to preserve their identity. Initially the Congress ventilated vitriolic opposition to this obnoxious principle. But it appears that the compulsions of political forces active at that time might have induced it to accept partition as a political solution to arrest the communal holocaust, without endorsing the two-nation theory in principle. Thus the two-nation theory was a prominent source of tension between Hindus and Muslims and it resulted in the nettled relationship between India and Pakistan.

## Congress Muslim League Divergence

The interplay of virulent political forces and a tug-of-war between the Congress and the Muslim League played a vital role in the events leading to partition. The establishment of Congress in 1885 and the Muslim League in 1906 marked the beginning of a new chapter in the socio-political history of India. The inter-party interaction between the two parties which was characterized by an intense quest for power and a crisis of identity shaped the course of events leading to the split of the sub-continent.

The ideological divergences between the two turned so implacable that unison between them became preposterous. The politics of separatism practised by the Muslim League and the dominant approach displayed by the Congress, generated an intense political heat and social tensions, which culminated in the horrendous events of 1947. Pandron Moon viewed: "There opened between the League and the Congress a breach destined to grow ever wider and to lead inexorably to the partition of the country and the massacres of 1947."[7]

The colonial rule in India has had a historic role in vandalising the multi-cultural edifice of the subcontinent. The wrecking tactics adopted by the imperial administration created a cleavage in the multi-cultural structure of Indian society and fomented separatist tendencies. After the British countered the united revolt of the Hindus and Muslims in 1857, the colonial Government apprehended the perils of Hindu-Muslim unity for their own existence. Hence they engaged in activities to rupture their unity. The first expression of this policy was seen when Lord Curzon divided Bengal in 1905. "The partition of Bengal was devised to divide people on the basis of religion and put Muslims against the Hindus."[8]

The next significant development in the sequel of events leading to the partition is the demand for separate electorate for Muslims. When Lord Morley and Lord Minto, were in the process of introducing constitutional reforms in India, a delegation led by Agha Khan demanded separate electorate for Muslims. Though initially Lord Morley turned down the demand, later Lord Minto realised its advantage for the British imperial ambitions and convinced Lord Morley and the proposal was accepted as a tool to propitiate the Muslims. Thus a separate electorate for Muslims was introduced in the constitutional reforms of 1909.

Even after this, there was no bluster for a separate homeland for Muslims. The unity between the two communities remained unblemished. But the British action had done substantial damage. Although, the Lucknow Pact "had succeeded in bringing the Congress and Muslim League together to a common platform to fight the British."[9] And this unity was demonstrated at the time of Khilafat and Non-Co-operation Movements.

But in the 1920s the divide between the two communities widened and signs of a budding strife, began to appear. "Never before communal question assumed such dangerous dimensions in the country, as it did in the 1920s."[10] The publication of Nehru report was a catalyst to this effect. This report counseled for obliterating the provisions relating to separate electorate and reservation of seats for Muslims. It proposed a federal form of Government for India but weighted heavily in favour of a strong centre. It was conspicuous that it did not merit admiration from either the Muslim League or the All India Muslim Conference. The Muslim leaders articulated that Nehru report manifested Hindu domination and it has been considered as the doom of Hindu Muslim synergy.

The blueprint of a separate homeland for Muslims first appeared in the 1930s in the leaflet published by a young undergraduate student of Cambridge, Rehamat Ali. His friends called it 'now or never'. In this Rahamat Ali coins the name Pakistan as a land of the pure for Muslim settlement and to celebrate Islamic way of life. His cartographic illustration of Pakistan consisted of the Punjab, Afghanistan, North Western Frontier Province, Kashmir, Sindh and Baluchistan.

It is pertinent to observe that even at this juncture the geo-political map of Pakistan remained nebulous. As aptly pointed out by Mushirulla Hasan: "There was, after all, no blueprint of a future Pakistan in the 1930s, no Islamic flag, no visible symbol, no common platform, no shared goals and objectives. Rehamat Ali's scheme nurtured in Cambridge was an illustration of obscurantism and political eccentricity. It caused much political embarrassment back home and was dismissed as chimerical and impractical."[11]

The grant of a separate electorate on communal lines which was proposed under the communal award issued by Ramsay MacDonald, the then Prime Minister of Britain, on August 4th 1932, in the wake of Constitutional reforms, accentuated the schisms between Hindus and Muslims. Mr. MacDonald corroborated his move on the basis that the two communities failed to arrive at a concordance. Thus "the communal award,

1932 of the British Government, further widened the gulf between the Hindus and Muslims."[12]

The period from 1937 to 1940 proved to be very critical in the history of the movement for Pakistan. This crucial period was a curtain raiser for a palpable idea of a separate Muslim homeland. The concept of Pakistan became clearer during this period. Muslim League emerged as the legitimate spokesman of a beleaguered community. During this time immense political heat was generated, due to the obduracy of the Congress to accept the League as the sole representative of Muslims in India.

Its refusal to form coalition Governments in the Hindu majority provinces, particularly the United Province, after 1937 elections, vexed the differences between the two communities. The Sindh Muslim League Conference of 1938 at Karachi, evolved a constitutional framework for the political independence of Muslims. This was the first organized expression of the separatist politics practised by the League. The All India Muslim League's Conference of 1940 was a turning point in the history of the movement for Pakistan.

The famous Lahore resolution of 1940, voiced its claims in favour of a separate homeland for Muslims. Commenting on the Pakistan resolution B. R. Ambedkar stated: "on 26th March 1940 Hindu India was startled to attention as it had never been before: on that day the Muslim League at its Lahore session passed a resolution. The resolution contemplates that the areas in which Muslims predominate shall be incorporated into independent States."[13] Lahore resolutions was an apparent declaration of the urge of Muslims for a separate homeland.

In August 1940 Lord Linlithgow offered a plan which is popularly known as the 'August Offer'. It proposed the setting up of a constitution making body with concrete assurance of full safety to the minority in any future constitutional arrangement. It received an applauding response from the League although the Congress reprehended it strongly and it launched the quit India movement which was also a protest against the Cripps mission.

The Muslim League did not support the movement and it exploited the situation for carrying out its own propaganda to mobilise Muslim opinion for the creation of a separate nation. In 1945 the Attlee Government sent a three-member mission called 'Cabinet Mission' consisting of British cabinet ministers. The mission aimed at negotiating with Indian leaders for framing a constitution and transfer of political power. Its plan endorsed the creation of a united India and vouched the complete safety of Muslims in it.

The mission devised a plan to create a three-tier political structure, consisting of the central Government, the regional unions and the provinces. According to it, India was to be divided into three major regions - section A consisted Madras, Bombay and UP, and section B consisted Bihar, Orissa, NWFP and Sindh. And section C consisted of Bengal and Assam. It proposed a central Government in charge of defense, communication and foreign affairs. The British created such a plan that anything could have been deduced from it.

Jinnah aspired to gratify a long cherished dream of the Muslims for a separate homeland and the Congress hoped to have a united India. The pre-condition of the plan was that the Indian leaders must accept ministerial offices in the responsible Government formed under the plan with a proposal to create two Muslim majority provinces with full autonomy.

This seemed to satisfy the demand of the Muslim League to a considerable extent. They anticipated the creation of a separate homeland for Muslims and they accepted the plan. On the other hand, the Congress opposed the plan, because, according to it, grouping of provinces was mandatory. The Congress Government was functioning in NWFP which would be shifted to section B and the Hindu majority province of Assam was to be shifted to section A which was not acceptable to the Congress.

So the Congress accepted the proposal but demanded that the grouping of provinces must not be obligatory.

This made the Muslim League to withdraw from the plan and it observed the 'direct action day' under the leadership of Jinnah. This was the last nail to the coffin and all hopes of bringing together the two communities dwindled, the prospects of India emerging free and united petered out and the partition of India became more likely.

The movement for Pakistan was authenticated when in 1946 the Muslim League adopted a Pakistan resolution in Karachi. This event ignited communal frenzy that ultimately culminated into the horrendous events of 1947 and the mass migration which was unfamiliar to human history. At this moment India was on the verge of a civil war, even the Congress which championed the idea of united India, came to terms with the degenerating communal situation and the destabilisation of the socio-political order.

At this grave moment, Lord Mountbatten came to India and "On 23rd March the Muslim League observed the 'Pakistan day'."[14] Mountbatten came to an inevitable conclusion that the only solution for the political impasse prevailing in India was partition. Subsequently, the V.P Menon plan was framed containing modalities for the partition. Lord Mountbatten got it approved by the British Government.

The essence of V. P. Menon plan was that the provinces of Punjab and Bengal were to be divided to create Pakistan. To ascertain the popular verdict the issue was to be placed before the legislative assemblies of the two provinces on the condition that if any one assembly votes in favour of partition both the provinces were to be divided. The question of NWFP was to be decided on the basis of referendum. So was the case with the Muslim majority district of Syllehat. The position of Sindh was to be decided by a special meeting of the legislative assembly of Sindh.

The issue was put to vote in the assemblies and they voted in favour of Pakistan. The referendum in NWFP went in favour of Pakistan and the same was the case with Syllehat. A special meeting of the legislative assembly of Sindh decided to join Pakistan. As soon as the plan was prepared Lord Mountbatten broadcasted it before the nation on June 3rd. Hence this is known as 'June 3rd plan'. Though the plan met with adverse criticism, it was accepted as an inevitable evil. A boundary commission was appointed under the chairmanship of Sir Cyril Radcliff in order to demarcate the geographical limits of both the countries.

On 4th July 1947 the independence of India bill was introduced in the British parliament and it was passed by a majority and the independence of India act came into existence on 18th July. It provided for the creation of two independent and sovereign nations, India and Pakistan and the British colonial links were to be dismantled. This act came into force on the appointed date of 15th August 1947, ending approximately two hundred years of colonial rule.

Thus the appalling events which marked the course of events leading to the partition of the sub-continent, engraves in itself the genesis of Indo-Pakistan antagonism. "The traumatic days of partition undoubtedly left behind deep scars on both sides, but an explanation of Indo-Pakistan hostility is limited to that short period in the life of an ancient land at once begs a broader and more fundamental question. What deep-seated compulsions caused the Hindus and Muslims to split the sub-continent which geographically forms a single unit."[15]

## *References*

1. J.N. Dixit, *India-Pakistan in War and Peace,* India Today Group, New Delhi, 2002, p. 102.

2. Ravi Nanda, Colonel, AVSM, *Indo-Pak Detente,* Lancer Books, New Delhi, 1989, p. 21.

3. Sumit Ganguly, *Conflict Unending,* Oxford University Press, New Delhi, 2002, p. 2.

4. Ashwini, K. Ray, *Domestic Compulsions and Foreign Policy: Pakistan in Indo-Soviet relations 1947-58*, Manas Publication, New Delhi, 1975, p.9.

5. Mushoirul, Hasan, *Introduction to India's Partition Process : Strategy and Mobilisation,* Oxford University Press, New Delhi, 1997, p. 9.

6. Navnita Chadha, Behera, India Pakistan Relations : Alternative Foreign Policy Options, in Lalit Mansingh ed., *India's Foreign Policy Agenda for the 21st Century* Vol. 2, Konark publishers, New Delhi, 1997, p. 236.

7. Penderel Moon, *Divide and Quit*, Oxford University Press, New Delhi, 1998, p. 11.

8. B. L. Grover and S. Grover, *A New Look at Modern Indian History,* S. Chand and Co., New Delhi, 1998, p. 309.

9. Hamza Alavi, Social Forces and Ideology in the Making of Pakistan, *Economic and Political Weekly,* 37(51), December 21, 2002, p. 4066.

10. V.N. Datta, Iqbal, Jinnah and India's Partition – An Intimate Relationship, *Economic and Political Weekly,* 37(50), December 14, 2002, p. 3898.

11. Mushoirul, Hasan, Supra, No. 5, p. 14.

12. B.L. Grover and S. Grover, Supra, No. 8, p. 595.

13. B.R. Ambedkar, *Pakistan or Partition of India,* Thacker Publications, Bombay, 1945, pp. 3-4.

14. V.D. Mahajan, in Dow Dall, [Ed.], *Cambridge History of India,* S. Chand and Company, New Delhi, 1979, p. 846.

15. S.M. Burke and Lawrence Ziring, *Pakistan's Foreign Policy: A Historical Analysis,* Oxford University Press, Karachi, 1990, p. 4.

Chapter 4

# The Unending Conflict

"The story of Indo-Pakistan relations is by and large one of the mutual animosity and confrontation, though there were agreements on some issues."[1] In a short span of about six decades, the two neighbours have fought four wars and concluded several agreements, but they have proved to be futile in terms of improving their bilateral relations. Many bilateral disputes have been solved or they are on the verge of being resolved. "but the winds of change seem to have bypassed the sub continent."[2]

India and Pakistan are the pillars upon which the affairs of South Asia rests. Their relations have a profound impact over the socio-economic and political spheres of the entire region. Primarily due to the Indo-centric character of the region, "Indo-Pakistan relations have been a major factor in the politics of South Asia and through it in the power politics of the world."[3]

India is the largest and most developed country in South Asia and Pakistan shares with it a common history, culture, geographical similarities and common economic problems which warrant co-operation between the two. Prolific collaboration between India and Pakistan will facilitate a greater role for both in world affairs. Zafrulla Khan, the first foreign secretary of Pakistan, remarked: "Pakistan and India if stood together could play in world affairs almost a decisive role."[4]

However it is regrettable that India Pakistan relations are marked by a state of mutual antipathy and ultimately South Asia has become a hot bed of intrigues and a hub of super power politics. In view of these considerations, it is pertinent to understand the major events that have occurred in the last nearly six decades. Perhaps, this will help to analyse the complex problems of India-Pakistan relations.

## Problems Arising out of Partition

After independence, India and Pakistan faced a number of problems because "British India broke up in haste since the U.K. was then exhausted after the Second World War and the former imperialists had only one thought to get rid of huge India's endless problems."[5]

The leaders of Pakistan advocated partition on the plank of 'two-nation theory', but the Congress leaders spurned it, and accepted partition as a compromise to end the communal holocaust. Actually, the British Government did not take any expedient measures to deal with the problems such as communal riots, demographic shifts, problems of minorities, demarcation of boundaries, disposal of evacuee property and sharing of assets and military.

The primary question was of demarcation of the boundaries of Punjab and Bengal, in order to stipulate the geographical limits of both the countries. For this purpose an Indo-Pakistan boundary commission was appointed, under the chairmanship of Sir Cyrill Radcliff on 30th June 1947. The commission gave its report on 12th August 1947, which, in turn, led to several problems. To solve these, the Indo-Pakistan boundary disputes tribunal was set up with Alghat Buggi as its chairman. The Buggi awards were published in 1950 and both the countries accepted them.

## First Kashmir War

One of the most ruffled territorial disputes that has had a

significant impact upon the security situation of South Asia and augurs adverse ramifications for global affairs is the Kashmir issue. The bilateral dispute between India and Pakistan regarding their geo-political claims upon the territory of Jammu&Kashmir has a major bearing on the defence and foreign policy of both. The imbroglio ushered in, as a result of partition, as the British left India with a legion of partition problems.

After the end of British rule, Kashmir had remained an independent princely state. Pakistan, since beginning nurtured an irredentist policy towards Kashmir. Meanwhile in October 1947 there was a tribal insurrection in Poonch region of Kashmir. The Pakistan army nabbed the opportunity and finessed an intrusion into the territory. The security forces of the crown were not competent enough to counter tribal incursions backed by the Pakistani army. In such a predicament, Raja Hari Singh approached the Government of India for help.

After the king signed the instrument of accession, the Indian military was deployed for operations in Kashmir. An open war began between the armies of India and Pakistan. At this juncture, India took the matter to the UN, and the latter ordered for immediate halting of the militaries of both countries and declared a cease-fire in Kashmir. In the meantime, the intruders were able to hold on to approximately 33% of the territory in Kashmir and declared it as Azad Kashmir (free Kashmir). The Pakistan Government backed the revolutionaries to establish an interim Government in Azad Kashmir and since then the territory is under the indirect control of Pakistan Government.

This event paved way for the emergence of a prominent issue which has jeopardized peaceful relations between India and Pakistan. Even after more than six decades of their existence Kashmir remains a labyrinth. The nature of defence and foreign policy of both India and Pakistan is determined by the matrix of their bilateral relations which in turn is predicated upon one single issue that is Kashmir. All other problems, like terrorism and nuclear arms race are the appendage of Kashmir conundrum.

## Pakistan's Military Alliance with the US and Indo-Pakistan Relations:

Cold war politics started influencing Indo-Pakistan relations after Pakistan joined the U.S. sponsored military alliance in 1953. The Pakistani decision was entirely against the fundamental principles of India's foreign policy, which centered on non-alignment that advocated an independent foreign policy characterised by non-involvement in power blocks and non-participation in wars. But with Pakistan's decision to join the military alliance, the flames of cold war permeated into the parameters of South Asia. Pakistan's move compelled India to upgrade its military strength and divert its resources from development to defence.

The Pakistani action might be the offshoot of its urge to acquire military parity with India and it appears that the "failure to solve Kashmir issue had brought about a US-Pakistan military agreement in 1953 and had presented a threat to the whole of South Asia."[6] Apart from this the "Primary motivation for Pakistan's alliance may have been the internal factors of the country, rather than its foreign policy needs."[7] Whatever may be the impulse stimulating the Pakistani policy decision, it brought serious ramifications on the nature of Indo-Pakistan relations, which provoked a fierce arms-race between India and Pakistan that ultimately culminated in both the countries declaring their nuclear capabilities in 1998 and indicated candid motives for nuclear weaponization.

## Sino-Indian War of 1962 and Indo-Pakistan Relations:

"In Indo-Pakistan relations China too fell out with India and Indo-Pakistan relationship became a part of Sino-Indian syndrome."[8] In 1962 there was a war between India and China on the Aksai Chin, which had long ranging repercussions on the politics of the Sub-continent. It shook the roots of India's core doctrine of Non alignment and jolted the principle of Panchasheel, which was the cornerstone of Sino-Indian relations. The war also unmasked the weakness in India's defense policy.

A serious need for the structural re-orientation of India's defence and foreign policy was felt, as India's weakness could prove to be an advantageous situation for Pakistan. India's debacle in the war gave Pakistan an opportunity to re-examine the direction and objectives of its foreign policy. Now it began to importune China for military and strategic assistance and the latter reciprocated. It started to support Pakistan on various issues of India-Pakistan relations, for instance, "although the Peoples Republic had not, at that time, made its view point on Kashmir clear in any official statement up to 1962, it leaned towards Pakistan's claim"[9] The Sino-Indian conflict indirectly contributed to the worsening of India Pakistan relations and was "partly responsible for their clash in 1965."[10]

**Dispute over the Rann of Kutch:**

The Western border of India with Pakistan begins at the mouth of the river Sir Creek. There is a dispute over the first 104 kms of the border. India contends that the border should be at the median of the navigable channel of the river. Pakistan asserts that the border should be along the left bank of the river. The area between Gujarat and West Pakistan along the western border separating India and Pakistan is known as the Rann of Kutch. "The great Rann extends from a north- south line for about 400 kilometers."[11]

Since partition there was a dispute between India and Pakistan over the Rann of Kutch. It snowballed into an armed conflict in 1965. Pakistan took the opportunity and exploited the instability created due to the war at the western front and extended the war to Kashmir. Pakistan did this on the notion that, after the Hazratbal incident the situation in Kashmir was volatile and it could be maneuvered for its own advantage. However, the hostilities in the Rann of Kutch were ended due to the good offices of the British Prime Minister, Herald Wilson, and India and Pakistan concluded an agreement in June 1965. A ceasefire arranged by the U.N. ended the war in Kashmir. Thus the 21 day war between India and Pakistan ended in an impasse, with the parties failing to gain any mileage from it.

## Tashkent Agreement of 1966

After the wrangle at the western front the relations between India and Pakistan had gone into a cold storage and the process of building peace appeared to be very exacting. "The Tashkent meeting between Prime Minister Lal Bahadur Shastri and president Ayub Khan had been brought about by the dexterous diplomacy of the Soviet leaders."[12] Thus India and Pakistan signed the historic Tashkent agreement in 1966. "No doubt the Tashkent meet was a historic moment and with Soviet assistance a breakthrough had been achieved. An atmosphere of cautious optimism prevailed and for the first time some hope was entertained that India and Pakistan might be able to turn from the path of conflict and strive to live in amity and peace."[13]

But this was not to be. The peace process begun at Tashkent was derailed due to various reasons. At first cut, the divergence in the perceptions of India and Pakistan regarding the nature of Tashkent agreement was obvious. Although the 1965 war had ended in a stalemate with neither party gaining any vantage over its opposite camp but the relative superiority of Indian military capabilities as against that of Pakistan was clearly demonstrated in the war. This posed a principle challenge to the Pakistani ruling establishment and forced it to resort to greater imports of military hardware and sophisticated weapons from the US, USSR and China. In addition to this, an attempt was made to forge a triangular axis between the US, China and Pakistan, which would have been a grave threat to the security of South Asia. As a result, the diplomatic ties between India, China and Pakistan were strained. The relations between the two dropped to a wretched position only to be revitalized after the Shimla agreement.

**Indo-Pakistan War of 1971**

There was an apparent difference between the wars of 1948, 1965 and the war of 1971. Whereas in the previous conflicts war was caused due to the initiative by Pakistan compelled by a flawed inference regarding its claims on Kashmir. But the antecedents of the third armed conflict of 1971 were engraved in the domestic politics of Pakistan and the failure of the federal set up within its polity.

Pakistan consisted of two wings-East Pakistan and West Pakistan. The East Pakistan primarily contained a population dominated by ethnic Bengali stock, while the population of West Pakistan was primarily Urdu speaking. There was a persistent Bengali-Urdu dichotomy, since the inception of Pakistan. On the other hand, the regional disparity between the Eastern and the Western part of Pakistan was glaring. East Pakistan was a neglected region. The resource allocation was tilted in favour of the Western wing and the pinnacle of political power, administration and military in Pakistan was dominated by men from West Pakistan. All this ushered in a strong urge for autonomy in East Pakistan.

The general elections of 1970 conducted for both the national assembly of Pakistan and the provincial assembly of East Pakistan, produced phenomenal results. A landslide victory in both national and provincial assembly was achieved by the Awami League of East Pakistan headed by Sheikh Mujibur Rahman. But both the military junta and the Pakistan People's party headed by Z. A. Bhutto, declined to accept the poll verdict. Bhutto's obstructionism and non co-operation impeded the commencement of the democratically elected Government under the leadership of Sheikh Mujibir Rahman. Bhutto argued that the Government should be formed on the basis of a power sharing arrangement in a coalition Government of Pakistan People's Party and Awami League. But this was not acceptable to the leaders of East Pakistan.

In the mean time, widespread demonstrations and protests began in East Pakistan. General Yahya Khan declared marshal law and the situation became grievous, leading to a full-scale civil war. The Pakistani Government launched a military crack-down in the name of 'operation search light'. 'The operation' was mainly directed towards the Bengalis of East Pakistan. The military took recourse to ruthless violence, which resulted in the open declaration of the liberation movement by Sheikh Mujibur Rahman and he called for the creation of an independent country Bangladesh.

At this juncture, there was a heavy influx of refugees from East Pakistan into the Indian territories bordering it. It is estimated that nearly ten million refugees were found in its north-eastern States. This threatened the socio-economic and political stability of India and put the country's national security in serious jeopardy. India pressed Pakistan through diplomatic channels to bring a solution to the problem. But its admonitions went unheard. In such a precarious situation where all the options had been depleted, Indian leadership decided to favour East Pakistan's claims and resorted to military action, against Pakistan, purely in the interest of safeguarding its national security.

Thus what was purely a domestic problem of Pakistan, got transformed into an open war between India and Pakistan. In the ensuing war, India's military victory over Pakistan also ensured the liberation of East Pakistan and the emergence of the sovereign State of Bangladesh. With the defeat of Pakistan the ideology of 'two-nation theory' which was the foundation upon which Pakistan was created was startled leading to the debilitating of Pakistan's claims on Kashmir. On the other hand, the demonstration of India's military superiority as against that of Pakistan rendered any military offensive from Pakistan to be incredible.

**Shimla Agreement of 1972**

To arrive at a post-war settlement, the prime minister of India Mrs. Indira Gandhi and president of Pakistan Z. A. Bhutto met at the summit meeting in Shimla which took place from June 28 to July 2, 1972. The Indian objectives for the summit aimed at persuading Pakistan to accept bilateralism as the sole mechanism for figuring out all outstanding disputes, refurbishment of diplomatic ties which were dismantled in 1969, repatriation of the prisoners of war and Pakistani approbation to the principle that all existing frontiers with India are impregnable.

Pakistan went to the summit with the following key objectives-(1) to secure the release of 93,000 Pakistani prisoners of war and prevent Bangladesh from holding trials upon them for war crimes. (2) To recover 5,000 sq miles of its territory which it had lost to India in the western sector and (3) ensure that it's long standing position on Kashmir dispute was not basically mutated. The bilateral dialogue in Shimla, resulted in substantial success for both the parties. The agreement paved way for the repatriation of prisoners of war and restoration of diplomatic ties between the two countries. It was agreed that bilateralism would be the chief mechanism for resolving all contentious issues. One of the most significant outcome, of the summit is that after pledging themselves to abjure from use of force in finding a favourable solution to Kashmir issue, the two sides agreed to reaffirm the 1948 cease-fire line dividing POK and the mainland of Kashmir into the line of control and they agreed to transform it to a *de jure* international border.

In the Shimla talks, Bhutto assured his Indian counterpart that he would take active steps to integrate POK and other parts of the erstwhile princely State of Kashmir which were on the side of Pakistan into its federal setup. Hence, in over a quarter of a century of the history of Indo-Pakistan relations, which were characterised by hostilities and belligerent foreign policies, Shimla agreement was the most sanguine event. An aura of optimism dawned in South Asia which up till now was lackadaisical under the darkness of antagonism. But this was not to last for long. Until Bhutto was in power, He remained obstinate upon the Shimla agreement. But during the regime of General Zia-ul-Haq the spirit of Shimla agreement was not considered seriously in the making of Pakistan's foreign policy. Consequently, there appeared a gradual degeneration of the cordiality in India Pakistan relations.

## Pakistan's Proxy War in Kashmir

Pakistan's fiasco to fulfill its cherished dreams of merging Kashmir into its territory, even after three open wars induced the political class in Pakistan to espouse odious methods for accomplishing the task which remained incomplete at the time of the great divide. Demonstration of the Indian military superiority in these wars acclimatised the convictions of the Pakistanis that, acquisition of Kashmir from India through a conventional military confrontation is a remote contingency. Hence Pakistani policy makers decided in favour of an unconventional warfare and launched a proxy war against India in Kashmir.

For this Pakistan devised a two-pronged strategy. Initially the aim was to exert pressure along the LOC by intense trance-border firing. Then the objective was to encourage large-scale infiltration and sabotages at vital places in Kashmir. All this was directed to destabilize India internally and create an aura of insecurity in the region. The key objective of Pakistan's strategy was to wage a low intensity war; the degree of violence in the war was calibrated on the lower side, in order to facilitate a low cost and a less risky war which would not transform into a full scale war. Pakistan wanted the nature of proxy war to be protracted, the aim being to demoralise Indian security forces and erode their conventional military superiority by their ceaseless engagement in counter-insurgency operations.

Pakistani initiative to procure nuclear weapons has been a great stimulus which has animated its policy makers to mould such military strategies in order to realize their cherished goals. The ISI has been playing a vital role in the ongoing proxy war in Kashmir. The intelligence agency of Pakistan had gained immense proficiency in organizing guerrilla warfare through terrorism and sabotage as options and it is now involved in funding and training militant groups to carry out terrorist activities in Kashmir. "The low intensity conflict continues unabated since Pakistan sponsored militancy first erupted in Kashmir valley in 1989-1990 and cries of Azadi [independence] rent the air. Pakistan's aim is to destabilise India by all possible means. Protracted proxy war and sustained political and diplomatic offensives are part of a well-crafted strategy to keep India in internal squabbles and impose a heavy burden on Indian economy."[14]

Due to Pakistan's nefarious designs India has to pay a heavy price in terms of civil and military casualties and today catastrophe and insecurity have become the order of the day in Kashmir. But for all this only Pakistan cannot be blamed. It is "self evident that a foreign power can sow the seeds of insurgency only when discontentment and descent are wide spread among the people and the situation is ripe for exploitation. Due to decades of poor governance, neglect, compounded by rampant corruption, cynical nepotism, alienation from national mainstream and political mismanagement, the situation in Jammu and Kashmir was as bad as could possibly have been in 1988-1989."[15]

## Indo-Pakistan Relations in the Post Cold War Period:

The end of Second World War signaled the commencement of a cold war between the two super powers of the times; The US and the USSR. For nearly five decades global affairs were dominated by these two super powers. Indo-Pakistan relations did not remain secluded from the dynamics of Cold War politics. When Pakistan joined the military alliance with the US, South Asia was enveloped in the mist of cold war. The massive military assistance proffered to Pakistan by the US, compelled India to upgrade its defence capability in the light of its security interests. This appears to be one of the primary reasons for the growth of an arms race between India and Pakistan and engulfing the politics of the sub-continent into a cold war paradigm.

The relatively favourable posture of the US towards Pakistan in the matters of issues concerning Indo-Pakistan relations instigated India to look towards the USSR for support. In this regard, the Indo-Soviet treaty of peace, friendship and co-operation invigorated the cementing of bonds between the two countries. After this, India received an unflinching support from the USSR, specifically in matters relating to its disputes with Pakistan.

The expression of the positions of the two super powers apropos India-Pakistan affairs can be seen in the Indo-Pakistan war of 1971. During the war America expressed solidarity with Pakistan and threatened India's coast line by naval action in the wake of India taking recourse to military action against Pakistan. The Soviet Union pledged to retort this by military action, for the protection of India's security interests. This implies that both the super powers sided with either disputed parties, primarily for attaining mileage over the other. Their diametrical positions in the Security Council over Indo-Pakistan affairs, exemplifies their leanings.

The involvement of the two super powers in the affairs of Indo-Pakistan relations was purely motivated by their own self interests. One of the reasons for the US forming a military alliance with Pakistan was to build the latter as a regional surrogate to curb the Soviet expansion in the region and not to build it against India. In the same way the Soviet support to India seems more to be a counter reaction to the American action rather than its interests in the issues of Indo-Pakistan relations. However, it can be noted that both super powers remained neutral in their stance regarding Kashmir issue.

The demise of the Soviet Union terminated the turbulence

of cold war and recorded the opening up of a new chapter in the political history of modern world. The end of cold war brought about systemic changes in international politics, the bipolar international system was transformed into a unipolar world with America emerging as the sole super-power. In view of this, it was speculated that Indo-Pakistan relations would witness qualitative changes. But it is a paradox that the texture of bilateral relations of India and Pakistan remains the same, characterised by unmitigated hostilities. This has happened because the impact of cold war on the contentious bilateral issues of India and Pakistan such as Kashmir issue was not historic. However, America continues to be influential in the affairs of South Asia to a considerable extent. After the collapse of USSR, severe domestic bottlenecks have precluded Russia, from an active engagement in the chemistry of Indo-Pakistan relations. The pendulum now swings towards a triangular relationship between India, Pakistan and the US.

After the end of cold war, a basic shift was sighted in the American policy towards South Asia, because now in the changed environment the US did not need Pakistan as a regional surrogate for its anti-communist operations and it is expected that America will have an unbiased attitude towards the issues of Indo-Pakistan relations and there are some positive signs in this direction. Firstly, when India and Pakistan conducted nuclear tests, America displayed an unprejudiced approach when it was square enough to equally condemn and impose sanctions against both India and Pakistan. Similarly, at the time of Kargil crisis, American support to India was specific and Pakistan was reprehended for violating the LOC.

But American economic interests in West and Central Asia are still keeping it tilted towards Pakistan for logistical and strategic support. This was evident when Pakistan played a significant role as a base for US operations in Afghanistan, after the September 11 terrorist attacks. An American interest in Afghanistan is likely to continue as the latter can play a strategic role in the enterprises of the US in West and Central Asia. In this regard, Pakistan has a vital role as it provides logistical and strategic support to sustain American ventures. It can be inferred that in due course of time the US factor will be one of the significant ingredients in determining the nature of Indo-Pakistan relations in the changed international situation.

### Indo-Pakistan Relations after Nuclear Tests

The arrant animosities and an exasperated deadlock over the contentious issues of India and Pakistan have created a restive environment between the two countries. The hostilities, which sprung up at the time of partition of the sub-continent, persist as protracted and strained bilateral relations.

The political history of Indo-Pakistan relations is replete with an account of extravagant funding towards defence purposes, only to alleviate the threat perceptions from each other. Most of the problems of Indo-Pakistan relations have emerged as a result of the consternation engendered by the obsession regarding a menace to their security from each other, which constrained them to intensely weaponise and ameliorate their military strength. The paucity of confidence upon each other ushered in a cadaverous arms race between the two countries that has peaked into a nuclear arms race.

One of the primary causes for the nuclearisation of India and Pakistan was the stalemate over Kashmir which impelled Pakistan to resort to acquire nuclear capability in order to counter India's conventional military superiority. The course of the nuclearisation of sub-continent was in its embryonic stage when in the 1950s and 1960s leaders in Pakistan specially Z. A. Bhutto, embarked upon attaining nuclear capability in a search for its military applications for gaining preponderance over India to bring favourable solutions for Kashmir issue. The military defeat of Pakistan at the hands of India in 1971 and India's nuclear tests at Pokhran in 1974, acted as catalysts in accentuating the process of nuclearisation of Pakistan.

On the other hand, India encircled in a nuclear neighbourhood with China emerging as a declared nuclear power in 1964 and Pakistan having furtive nuclear capabilities was compelled to make endeavors to enhance its nuclear capacities to keep the nuclear weapon option open. Apart from this, the Sino-Pakistan nuclear axis simulated dire consequences for the security of India. In the 1980s there was a covert nuclear arms race between India and Pakistan and the undeclared nuclear status of the two caused much friction between them. A threat of a nuclear conflict loomed over the entire South Asian region due to Pakistan's constant intimidation to use its nuclear caliber. As a result of this, a veil of ambiguity cloaked the region.

However, the obscurity was terminated when India and Pakistan traversed the precincts and conducted nuclear tests in May 1998. India after a chronic ambiguity and constricted restraint outstripped the bounds and conducted five nuclear tests on May 11th and 13th 1998 at Pokhran, "signaling its entry into the exclusive club till now comprising five big powers. The people of India now have a credible nuclear deterrent, it was officially stated."[16]

The obvious aim of these tests was different from those of the tests carried out in 1974. While the official statement as claimed in 1974 indicated that the nuclear tests were conducted for peaceful purposes. But the Government's position after the Pokhran II nuclear tests was explicit in declaring India's genuine security compulsions that galvanise the tests which were directed towards a search for a minimum credible nuclear deterrence.

In the mean time, for Pakistan achieving military parity with India was the primary motivation driving its defence and foreign policy, right from its inception. India's Pokhran II nuclear test was a major challenge for the policy makers and strategists in Pakistan. Consequently, Pakistan did not desist from exhibiting its nuclear capacity and it carried out six nuclear tests in the third week of May 1998, at Chagai range in Baluchistan province.

The nuclear testing by India and Pakistan has brought long lasting implications for their defence and foreign policies. It has further complicated the nature of their bilateral relations. The immediate effect of the tests was the emergence of a threat of a nuclear war in the region. This event prognosticates an arms race between the two countries, rendering the contentious issues between them to become more intricate.

The Kashmir issue also has assumed critical dimension and the region has been dubbed as a nuclear flash point. "One of the conspicuous consequences of the nuclear blasts by India on May 11 and 13, 1998 and by Pakistan later is internationalisation of Kashmir issue."[17] Nuclear weapons have become a new source of tension between India and Pakistan and the event revitalises the fact that mistrust and misconception are the fundamental tenets governing the ruffled Indo-Pakistan relations. So "Nuclear explosions detonated by India and Pakistan, changed the geo-strategic environment in the region. These explosions will have far reaching effects at the regional and global level."[18]

**Bus Diplomacy**

In the 1990s the amplitude of discord between India and Pakistan intensified owing to several reasons. Significantly the outbreak of militant activities ushered in with the proxy war of Pakistan in Kashmir, leading to further deterioration of the situation in the valley. The dialogue process also was rendered to be atrophy, due to the outbreak of the proxy war. Moreover, nuclear testing by India and Pakistan and the subsequent developments further pushed the bilateral relations between the two countries, to a dejected and a squalid posture.

In this crucial moment the then BJP led coalition Government under the leadership of prime minister A B Vajpayee took various confidence building and diplomatic measures to pacify the relations between India and Pakistan. The first significant step in this direction was the decision to start a bus service from

New Delhi to Lahore. The objective was not only to boost and uplift the declining stature of bilateral relations; it was also a diplomatic innovation, primarily to brace people to people contact and to bring uniformity of interest between citizens of the two countries.

The notion was that the new step would facilitate the citizens on both sides of the border to fathom the exact nature of disputes between their countries, so that a broad framework could be evolved for discovering feasible solutions to the exasperated conflict. "It was a very small step, but not less exciting, for that in a situation where in people-to-people contact, were snapped almost completely, its symbolic significance is not to be minimised."[19]

The ingenious step was positively received by Pakistan and after a few weeks of official deliberations, "India and Pakistan on 12th February 1999, signed a formal agreement for New Delhi-Lahore bus service."[20] The noble endeavor of the Indian Government was embellished with the announcement that the prime minister of India A. B. Vajpayee would travel to Lahore in the maiden run of the newly launched bus service and this became like icing cakes and cookies.

It was hoped that the little step taken in the right direction would make a soothing impact upon the complex milieu of Indo-Pakistan relations. It was felt that, "Prime Minister Atal Behari Vajpayee's bus trip to Lahore across the Attari Wagha border would mark the beginning of new dawn in Indo-Pakistan relations."[21]

## Lahore Declaration

The then prime minister, A. B. Vajpayee took the historic bus journey to Lahore and reached Lahore at 1600 hours on the 20th February 1999. In the 24 hours of his stay in Lahore, Vajpayee met not only the leaders of Pakistan but also engaged himself with the people of Pakistan.

In the meeting with his counterpart Nawaz Sharif, the Indian prime minister discussed various significant issues such as the dangers of nuclear accidents, military build-up along the borders and Kashmir issue. The talks culminated in the signing of Lahore declaration on 21st February 1999. The agreement as it stated: "The prime ministers of the republic of India and the Islamic republic of Pakistan, sharing a vision of peace and stability between their countries and the progress and prosperity of their people are convinced that the development of harmonious relations and friendly co-operation will serve the vital interests of the people of the two countries, enabling them to devote their energies for a better future."[22]

The declaration committed the two countries to take immediate steps to reduce nuclear accidents and unauthorised use of nuclear weapons. It also stated that the two countries will discuss principles and tenets for implementing confidence building measures in the ambit of both nuclear and conventional weapons capabilities in order to reduce conflicts. The declaration contained an assurance by both the countries regarding the no first use of nuclear weapons', striving for a no war pact, reduction of tension along the border and the peaceful resolution of Kashmir issue.

One of the immediate outcomes of Lahore declaration was that the then foreign secretaries of India and Pakistan, K. Raghunath and Shamshad Ahmad, signed a memorandum of understanding [MOU] in the presence of the two prime ministers. The memorandum expressed: "The two sides undertake to provide each other with advance notification in respect of ballistic missile flight tests and shall conclude an agreement in this regard."[23]

However, the Lahore process turned to be a fiasco. The jubilant optimism that dawned at the time when a bilateral agreement was reached between India and Pakistan at Lahore after a hiatus of over two decades was doomed in the recreant act of Pakistan in Kargil which again prostrated the geniality of relations between the two. As noted by Devesh Kapur: "At the end of 1999, India's relations with Pakistan were at a nadir not seen since 1971. The optimism that marked Vajpayee's historic Lahore visit in February 1999 proved short lived, when Pak intruders were found occupying the high mountains well within the Indian side of the line of control, in the Kargil sector of Kashmir."[24]

**The Kargil Crisis**

The relentless attempts of Pakistan to seize Kashmir persisted, even after it was vanquished to the hilt in 1971. The proxy war launched in Kashmir by Pakistan in the late 1980s reached the meridian, when Pakistan made a blatant attempt to physically occupy the strategic heights of Kargil sector in Kashmir valley. Pakistan's fourth war in Kashmir is a manifestation of its frenetic passion to change the geo-strategic position of India in Kashmir to its own advantage.

Pakistan's misadventure in Kargil came as a surprise to India, because after the signing of Lahore declaration, the perception in the Indian coterie and media was that Indo-Pakistan relations had been brought back on rails. But this proved to be a serious misunderstanding. The diplomatic initiative so magnanimously launched was in tatters when intruders perforated the line of control and captured the mountains of Kargil sector. The Pakistani Government keeping close nexus with militant groups of Kashmir forged a fractious venture in Kargil. Pakistani action in Kargil was dubbed by veteran South Asian observer Stephen Cohen as: "Brilliant militarily but disastrous politically caught India by surprise."[25]

One of the primary reasons for the outbreak of Kargil conflict is the truculent terrorist activities taking place in the region that created a war like situation. It demonstrated an escalation of the already existing tension. The Kargil intrusion does not connote a detached event. Infiltration across the line of control when the snow dissipates in the summer is not an unprecedented happening. "Nor the Kargil fixation of the Pakistani military is secret to the Indian armed forces and the intelligence set up. Since the war of 1971, shelling across the line of control has been a regular affair."[26] But the Kargil crisis was distinct from the regular intrusions because it was an obvious attempt made by Pakistani army to physically occupy the territory on the Indian side.

Some of the fundamental causes of Kargil crisis include the geographical difficulties of the region. It is one of the coldest and highest area in the world. Hence defence of Kargil poses a serious challenge to Indian security forces. Such bottlenecks have not only led to the recent Kargil crisis but the recurring of more Kargil type intrusions is always impending. Besides, the lacuna in India's intelligence set up and the failure of surveillance techniques have also been exposed.

But it is a contorted view that the outbreak of conflict in Kargil was basically due to the failure of intelligence. It seems that the lack of co-ordination between the administration, military and intelligence contributed to the Kargil crisis. Above all, the most significant cause was that the intuitions of Indian elite regarding the motives of Pakistan were inaccurate. The Indian coterie demonstrated a lack of insight when it was in a hallucination that after the Lahore peace initiative and the declared nuclear status of both the countries, Pakistan would not engage in a military venture with India. But this proved to be perfidious and India again confronted with an unprovoked incursion in Kashmir.

The Indian military in liaison with the air force launched a severe offensive against the intruders. The operation Vijay as it was called, aimed at driving out the intruders without crossing the line of control and ensuring that the issue was not internationalised. Hence the Indian army maintained strict military restraint. Thus, after nearly three months of military operation the Indian security forces were able to drive out the intruders and recapture the seven strategic heights of Kargil sector.

But for this, the nation had to bear a heavy loss in terms of the lives of soldiers and it imposed a severe economic burden upon the country. Indicating this, the Indian prime minister stated: "Operation Vijay was a great success fought at the cost of approximately 400 dead and over 600 injured. We owe it to these martyrs to learn from the mistakes made, so that assaults on our sovereignty do not become a recurring feature."[27]

In the Kargil crisis India not only achieved a military victory, but it was also crowned with a diplomatic victory. The nation got an unequivocal support from the international community and its diplomacy and the policy of military restraint was widely acknowledged. On the other hand, Pakistan received a scathing response for its defiant action in Kargil and was severely condemned for its infernal war crimes, disrespecting the LOC, augmenting tension on the border, profaning the spirit of Shimla accord and the Lahore declaration and it was diplomatically isolated. Thus, the Kargil crisis was a trouble turned into a boon for India, in terms of international support that it was able to garner, especially from the US.

The crisis brought complex implications for Indo-Pakistan relations. Due to the increased military build up, the tensions in Kashmir heightened. Above all, India lost all the faith it had on Pakistan because of its perfidy despite India's abiding exactions to promote peace in the region. The mood in the Indian coterie and public after the Kargil crisis can be summed up in the words of Muchkund Dubey, a former Indian foreign secretary: "India has taken a tough stand on resuming dialogue with Pakistan, it has been announced at the Prime Minister's level, that there would be no talks until Pakistan stops cross-border terrorism. Non-official quarters have even suggested the snapping of ties with Pakistan, including the withdrawal of the most favoured nation treatment to that country."[28] In the end, "Despite numerous similarities between the Indians and Pakistanis that favour a closer interaction and friendly ties between them, there are a few issues which have set them wide apart. Kashmir definitely ranks the top most among the subjects of discord between the two. Kargil has of late assumed a prominent position in the list of those matters, seeking to perpetuate Indo-Pakistan division."[29]

## The Agra Summit

The enduring efforts on the part of Indian Government to bring an amicable solution to the contentious disputes of India and Pakistan continued in spite of repeated failures. The air of pessimism which loomed over South Asia, after the tempest in Kargil and Lahore fiasco, was replaced with revived optimism when the then prime minister A.B. Vajpayee invited Pakistan president General Pervez Musharraf for a summit meeting in July 2001. Amidst an animated debate in the public, political circles and the media, regarding the rationale of holding the proposed summit in a moment when democracy in Pakistan was in shambles and the country was under international isolation after its Kargil misadventure, the prime minister boldly went ahead with his initiative.

The decision of the prime minister received lot of admiration and hopes were expressed that the summit would open new avenues for establishing a harmonious relationship between the two countries. But the antagonists debated the logic of holding a summit meeting with general Musharraf who had master minded the Kargil misadventure and he was also not a democratically elected head of State. So the validity of Musharraf as the leader of Pakistan was questioned. But these arguments did not stall the peace initiative and it was decided that the summit meeting would be held on 15th and 16th July 2001 at the historic city of Taj- Agra. The reason for holding the summit in Agra indicated the willingness of the Government to bring an atmosphere of informality to the deliberations of the summit.

The primary motivations driving the decision of Vajpayee led Government to invite Musharraf for a summit level meeting was diverse. "Prominent among them being the keenness to maintain continuity in peace process, after the Government's decision not to extend the cease-fire in the Kashmir valley, and pressures by the international community specially the US Government to initiate a dialogue with Pakistan that broke off after Kargil war."[30] For Pakistan President Mr. Musharraf the invitation was a boon in disguise as he got a much needed opportunity to prove the legitimacy of his regime and to show to his opponents at home and abroad that his regime was actively engaged in the direction of resolving the deadlock with India.

The Agra summit began with a high note on 15th July 2001. But there was mutiny abode that cast a shadow on the deliberations and debilitated the spirit of the summit. At the outset there was no unanimity between India and Pakistan over the issues to be discussed. If India emphasised that cross border terrorism is the prominent issue in the agenda for discussion Pakistan asserted upon the single point agenda of Kashmir. This divergent approach to the summit forestalled the signing of any joint declaration, at the end of the summit. The differences between the two countries over the issue of participation of Hurriyat in the summit also played its own part in jeopardizing the enthusiasm. While India opposed any third party entry in the dialogue process, Pakistan indicated its willingness to involve the Hurriyats in the summit by inviting them for tea party hosted by Pakistan's high commissioner.

Even after two days of intensive deliberations, India and Pakistan were not successful in bringing out a joint declaration, because of their differences over Kashmir and cross border terrorism and the summit had to be continued for the third day. But even this proved to be futile and the summit had to be called off without signing any agreement. The critics call the summit a failure, because India went into it without any structured agenda and that is why general Musharraf high-jacked it by his single point agenda of Kashmir and hence the peace initiative of Vajpayee Government was a failure.

But this was a myopic and pessimistic viewpoint. It can be said that the summit was not a failure but to put it in the words of India's former foreign minister Jaswanth Singh it was 'inconclusive'. The summit was not a total failure, its utility lies in the fact that it facilitated the maintenance of continuity in the peace process and provided a broad framework for future dialogue.

## Indo-Pakistan Relations after 11th September 2001

On 11th September 2001, the US was subjected to ghastly terrorist attacks in Washington, New York and Pennsylvania. It is reported that these terrorist strikes were masterminded by Osama Bin Laden who had the backing of Taliban regime of Afghanistan. When the US's requests to the Taliban to hand over the culprit were fruitless, it resorted to military action against the Afghan Government which led to the dismantling of Taliban regime. The event ushered in the reviving of US-Pakistan rapprochement, because the US required Pakistan for providing logistical and strategic support in its operations against Afghanistan.

Thus Washington indicated a tilt towards Islamabad and this was a golden opportunity for the military establishment in Pakistan as General Musharraf could get legitimacy to his military junta from the west. Further it was felt that the US-Pakistan relations, which had reached a nadir after Kargil crisis would be revitalized. Hence, Pakistan decided in favour of supporting the US operations in Afghanistan.

Indo-Pakistan relations did not remain uninfluenced by these developments in South Asia. After the global coalition against terrorism was formed under the leadership of the US, it was hoped that the situation in Kashmir would witness qualitative changes as the terrorist structures in POK would be dismantled and Pakistan would take concrete steps to end fomenting of terrorism from its soil. But it is an irony that no improvement has been sighted. The terrorist activities in various parts of India remain unremitting. Pakistan seems to have not come under the pressure of the US. Primarily due to U.S.'s preference for Pakistan, for the sake of preserving its own strategic interests in the region. There may also be a reincarnation of U.S. Pakistan military alliance that characterised South Asian politics in the entire period of cold war.

Thus the post September 11 scenario has brought intricate effects on the bilateral relations of India and Pakistan. In this regard, the triangular relationship between India, Pakistan and the US will be a major determinant of the nature of Indo-Pakistan relations in the future. The tensions between the two countries have been aggravated because of these antecedents and there is likelihood that the atmosphere in Kashmir may worsen, as there is every chance after the US operations in Afghanistan that the terrorists driven out of Afghanistan may permeate into Kashmir if Pakistan does not adopt adequate measures to avert such probabilities. Thus "The most conspicuous consequence was an upsurge of tensions in Kashmir, leading to clashes between India and Pakistan which have been locked in dispute over Kashmir for over 50 years."[31]

## Terrorist Attack on India's Parliament

On 13th December 2001 Indians were startled with a shock when the heart of Indian democracy and emblem of the country's sovereignty and strength, Parliament complex was attacked by five terrorists belonging to the Pakistan based militant outfits Jaish-e-Mohammed and Lashkar-e-Taiba. The event sent an air of consternation in the sub-continent and the two nuclear neighbours were on the verge of another lethal war the consequences of which were inconceivable. Indo-Pakistan relations that had been recovering from the jolt of Kargil crisis were exposed to a convulsion that perturbed all hopes of restoring an environment of cordiality between the two countries. The top leadership in India expressed anguish and there was an open pronouncement that the fight against terrorism had reached its final stage and the bounds of India's patience had been crossed.

The Indian government handed over a list of twenty terrorists who were suspected to be sheltered in Pakistan and demanded their immediate extradition. But Pakistan did not act in a manner that was desirable and Pakistan's procrastination exasperated Indian leadership. The ensuing events forced the weather between India and Pakistan reach to an ebb. "Both countries ordered the biggest mobilisation of their armies in fifteen years up to a total of one million troops on each side of the border."[32]

The international community including the US was shocked by the developments in South Asia. The Bush administration urged the leadership in New Delhi to maintain restraint. Although the international community expressed profound disquiet over the matter, it showed a sense of disclaimer. "In fact, India's attempts to build a persuasive case to the world community against Pakistan's sponsorship of terrorism appeared to evoke only lukewarm international resonance."[33]

Fortunately, for South Asia the situation did not flare up into a full scale war and Indian military build up only became a political brinkmanship without any desired outcomes. Instead it increased the economic burden because the centre had to incur heavy expenditure for stationing a mammoth army at the border. The event resulted in the severing of diplomatic ties between the two countries, with all links being blocked; including the Samjhauta Express, Delhi-Lahore bus service and air roots. The year 2002 was marked by rigorous military exercises on both sides of the border and heightened tensions. Anyway wise counsels prevailed and considerable demilitarisation on both sides led to gradual relaxation of the stress.

## Srinagar Peace Initiative

On April 18, 2003, the then Indian prime minister, Atal Behari Vajpayee, in the capital of Jammu and Kashmir Srinagar, retrieved the peace process which had been tumbled after the terrorist attacks on parliament and offered to hold a dialogue with Pakistan if the latter reciprocated by showing an inclination for discovering ways and means for attaining a lasting harmony between the two countries. The diplomatic move of the prime minister brought in renewed expectations on both sides and the step received a remarkably positive response from all quarters in India and Pakistan.

The then Indian Prime Minister, Vajpayee made a candid decision, considering the psychological torment which he had to undergo after the Lahore and Agra initiatives were miscarriaged. It was reported: "A dramatic transformation seemed to have come over the India-Pakistan discourse, with prime minister, Atal Behari Vajpayee's third and final call for friendship with Pakistan. What else one should make out over the threat of Vajpayee to retire if the peace move did not succeed."[34] The prime minister declared that this was his last bid to give peace a chance and to find an ultimate solution to bring amity in the region which is embroiled in a inveterate pugnacity between the two countries.

The Indian leadership which had borne an obstinate posture after the December 13 terrorist attacks and had declared that there will be no dialogue with Pakistan until cross border terrorism ended, displayed splendid ductility in offering the peace initiative. Both India and Pakistan were able to manumit themselves from their hard line positions and obsessions. There appeared a sensational change in the texture of relations between the two countries, from the probability of a collapse of diplomatic bonds and outbreak of a military conflict, to an emphasis to resolve all dominant issues with a realization that an overnight settlement of the contentious issues like Kashmir is impossible. Need was felt for devicing a step-by-step approach in order to bring a structured framework for a sustained dialogue.

The initial move in the peace process saw the declaration by the leaders of both the countries to restore diplomatic links, revive all transport connections and resume sports ties. However the dialogue process was very slow and the transport links, took a long time to resume. This was due to the perpetual series of terrorist violence in Kashmir and other parts of India, despite the process of constructive engagement.

To invigorate the peace process, the then BJP Government promulgated the Deewali Peace Offer, consisting a package of twelve confidence building measures drafted by the cabinet committee on security for normalising relations with Pakistan. "India took Pakistan and the diplomatic community based in New Delhi by surprise when it announced on October 22 2003, a 12-point proposal to resume the peace process with the neighbouring country."[35]

The proposed measures included, starting a bus service from Srinagar to Muzaffarabad [capital of Azad Kashmir], re-starting the Ferry service between Mumbai and Karachi which was stopped at the time of 1965 war and introduction of new rail/ bus service between Khokra-Par in Sindh and Munnabao in Rajasthan. The package spelt the desire on the part of Indian Government to start talks on the resumption of Samjhauta express and increasing the frequency of buses from Delhi to Lahore. Apart from this, the then Indian foreign minister, Yashwant Sinha proposed the setting up of a hotline between the coast guards of the two countries.

These were similar to the proposals made by the then Pakistani Prime Minister Mir Zafarullah Khan Jamali on May 6 2003 which had not been accepted by India. Jamali also had proposed for the increase of the frequency of Lahore-Delhi bus service. Anyway, Pakistan accepted the Indian package but with some controversial conditions. For instance, regarding Srinagar-Muzaffarabad bus service, Pakistan insisted that the check posts must be manned by UN forces and the people on both the sides must carry UN documents.

However, the differences have been resolved and the Bus service was successfully begun by the present Indian Government, reflecting the continuity in India's foreign policy, despite regime change. In addition to this, it has been proposed by the present Indian Prime Minister Manmohan Singh to connect two holy places, Amritsar in the Indian side of Punjab and Nankanasahib on the Pakistani side. Reacting to the change of guard at the center in India, Pakistan hoped: "It is expected of the new Government in India to take forward the peace initiative and work towards a resolution of all outstanding issues between the two countries including Jammu and Kashmir."[36]

The present Government has engaged in noble exertions to keep the peace process that was initiated by the previous Government headed by A.B. Vajpayee. This provides credence to the point that India's foreign policy is characterised by change and continuity. Despite the change in regime and a new Government with a different party in power, the fundamental tenets of the nations foreign policy remains intact. This also indicates that considerations of national interests have over determined partisan considerations, in the context of India's relations with Pakistan. The existence of common consensus among political parties on crucial issues of foreign policy is also evident.

Anyhow, in spite of all this, the basic character of India Pakistan relations has not been transformed. One of the primary reasons for this is the unrelenting terrorist violence which has been a major hurdle for the peace process. Terrorism still exists as a major factor that has contributed in magnifying the intricacies in their bilateral relations. "The July 11 terrorist attacks in Mumbai and the finger pointing towards Pakistan by India,"[37] signifies this notion. This event had a vicious impact on the diplomatic ties between the two countries, ultimately leading to the cancellation of the foreign secretary level meeting scheduled on 21st July 2006. The joint terror mechanism proposed by the leaders of the two countries at their meeting in Havana and the four point solution suggested by General Musharaff to resolve the Kashmir entanglement, have been described as chimerical. Hence India-Pakistan relations still remains in a labyrinth.

### References

1. A. Appadorai and M. S. Rajan, *India's Foreign Policy and Relations,* South Asia Publishers, New Delhi, 1972, p. 56.
2. Kalim Bahadur, India Pakistan Relations in 21st Century, *World Focus,* 226-227, 1998, p. 33.
3. Ashwini K. Ray, *Domestic compulsions and foreign policy: Pakistan in Indo-Soviet relations 1947-1958,* Manas publishers, New Delhi, 1975, p. 1.
4. M. Zafrulla Khan, cited in S. M.Burke and Lawrence Ziring, *Pakistan's foreign policy: a historical analysis,* Oxford University press, Karachi, 1990, p.3.
5. Lars Blinkenberg, *India-Pakistan, The History of Unsolved Conflicts, An Analysis of Some Structural Factors Vol II,* Odense University Press, Odense, 1999, p. 46.
6. Acharya Kripalni's statement, Parliamentary Debates, 10(20, 23 December 1953, Col. 3021, cited in *(Two Years of the Praja Socialist Party),* Praja Socialist Publication, Bombay, 1954, p. 31.
7. Ashwini K. Ray, Supra, No. 3, p. 55.
8. V. P. Datta, *India's Foreign Policy*, Vikas Publishing House, New Delhi, 1984, p. 137.
9. Denis Wright, *India-Pakistan Relations 1962-1969*, Sterling Publishers Private Limited, New Delhi, 1989, p. 9.
10. Ibid., pp. 9 and 40.
11. E. N. Ram Mohan, Disquiet on the Western Front, *Biiss Journal,* 133(552), April-June 2003, p. 59.
12. Kalim Bahadur, *Democracy in Pakistan Crisis and Conflicts*, Har-Anand Publications, New Delhi, 1998, p. 250.
13. V. P. Datta, Supra, No. 8, p. 141.
14. Alexander Evans, Talibanising Kashmir, *The World Today,* 57 (12), December 2001, pp. 14-15.
15. Gurmeet Kanwal, Proxy War in Kashmir : Jehad or State Sponsored Terrorism ?, *Strategic Analysis*, 23(1), April 1999, pp. 55-56.
16. The Hindu, 12th May 1998.
17. Balaraj Puri, A Post-Pokhran Policy for Kashmir, Economic and

*Political Weekly,* 33 (45), 7th November 1998, p. 2830.

18. Thehmina Mohmood, India and Pakistan's Nuclear Explosions : An Analysis, *Pakistan Horizon,* 52(1), January 1999, p. 48.
19. K.K. Katyal, The Hindu, 18th January 1999.
20. *The Times of India,* 18th February 1999.
21. Poonam Singh, Ira Yadav, Bus Trip to Lahore a Harbinger of Indo-Pak Co-operation in the Coming Millennium, *Review of Politics,* 7(1 & 2), January-June and July-December 1999, p. 55.
22. *The Hindu,* 22nd February 1999.
23. *The Hindustan Times,* 22nd February 1999.
24. Devesh, Kapur, India in 1999, *Asian Survey,* 40 (1), January-February 2000, p. 205.
25. Ibid., p. 204.
26. A. Bandhyopadhyaya, Kargil Conflict Causes, Liabilities and Solutions, *Third Concept,* 14 (161), July 2000, p. 1.
27. Vinod, Anand, India's Military Strategy in Operation Vijay, *World Focus,* 234-235, June-July 1999, p. 15.
28. Muchkund, Dubey, *The Hindu,* 20th August 1999.
29. *Our Task Today,* A Year After Kargil, [Editorial], *Mainstream,* 38(32), July 29, 2000.
30. P. S. Jayaramu, Vajpayee-Musharraf Summit Room for Cautious Optimism, *Mainstream,* 29(29), July 7, 2001, p. 6.
31. Pawel Milewski, Pakistan and India and the Events of September 11, *The Polish Quarterly of International Affairs,* Winter 2002, p. 123.
32. Ibid., p. 123.
33. Malini Parthasarathy, An Elusive Peace with Pakistan, *Seminar* 509, January 2002, p. 69.
34. Sukumar Muralidharan, A High-Stakes Initiative, *Frontline,* June 20, 2003, p. 24.
35. John Cherian, A Surprise Initiative, *Frontline,* 22 October, 8 November, 2003, p. 24.
36. *Asian News Digest,* May 31 June 6, 2004, 5(23), p. 3694.
37. The Editorial, *The Hindu,* July 12 2006.

Chapter 5

# Pakistan Factor in India's Foreign Policy: Perceptions of Political Parties

The Indian polity having a multi party system with a liberal character has been engrossed by political parties, in terms of policy processes, either domestic or foreign policy. As regards the motivational compulsions shaping India's foreign policy, it is needless to say that the perceptions and responses of major political parties regarding significant issues has been a crucial element. Political parties have provided a democratic character to the foreign policy making process by linking public opinion and policy makers. Hence the impact of the presence of political parties in crucial stages of the evolution of India's foreign policy has been decisive.

Concurrence of political parties on the dominant presence of the Pakistan factor is undebatable. Indo-Pakistan relations has assumed a dominant position in the realm of foreign affairs of both India and Pakistan. The climate of their bilateral relations, determines to a large extent their foreign policies. As a result Indo-Pakistan relations is a subject of immense interest in both the countries.

Even after six decades of their independence, their bilateral relations are unstable as they are marred by mutual antagonism. Regardless of the four wars and several agreements between the two countries, their relations does not seem to improve. Though there appear compromises, they tend to be ephemeral. Hence, Indo-Pakistan relations is a subject still left with a lot of scope for cogitating curative measures in order to discover methods for establishing lasting peace between the two countries.

In India, Indo-Pakistan relation occupy a position of pre-eminence in the ambit of its international relations and it constitutes a pivotal element of the country's defence and foreign policy. The field encompassing Indo-Pakistan relations has magnetized the cognizance of a wide range of segments in the Indian society comprising of scholars, journalists, interest groups and political parties. All have made an attempt to explore probable ways for resolving the nettled problem and have played their own part in the evolution of India's foreign policy towards Pakistan.

They constitute key domestic variables and their suggestions and recommendations have been one of the primary sources for deciding the fabric of India's foreign policy towards Pakistan. For the elites concerned with the enactment and execution of India's foreign policy, structuring a sagacious foreign policy to deal with this perplexed issue in the ambit of India's external affairs, poses a serious challenge.

In this regard, political parties as institutional mechanisms of the Indian political system have played a vital role in determining the texture of India's foreign policy towards Pakistan. Political parties determine the potency of responsiveness of Indian polity to counter challenges. India has to confront a lot of problems due to its ruffled relations with Pakistan. Here political parties' perception of the major issues of Indo-Pakistan relations is responsible for demarcating the contours of India's foreign policy towards Pakistan.

The foreign policy position of India is to a considerable extent decided by the nature of its relations with Pakistan. In this regard, the way in which political parties perceive the issues and problems of Indo-Pakistan relations will decide the capability of India to discover measures for instituting peaceful relations with its important neighbour. Thus it is pertinent to understand and analyse Indian political parties' perception and evaluation of the issues and problems of Indo-Pakistan relations in the broad framework of their position on India's foreign policy.

**Foreign Policy Position of the Indian National Congress**

The foreign policy position of the Congress party is the result of a long evolutionary process and not an outcome of an abrupt reaction. Congress party's foreign policy was formulated in the pre-independence period. History is a primary source of India's foreign policy which was moulded by prominent Congress leaders like Mahatma Gandhi and Pandit Nehru who laid down the fundamental tenets of India's foreign policy and shaped India's world view. The views of these leaders were conditioned by India's rich cultural heritage and its glorious history.

The nature and content of Congress's foreign policy can be traced back to its attitude towards various international issues expressed in the pre-independence period. The Congress party passed several resolutions articulating its views regarding various affairs of the British Indian Government outside the jurisdiction of India's cartographic limits. These resolutions not only delineate India's world views, but also mark out the primary objectives and principles of India's foreign policy such as non-alignment, anti-imperialism, anti-racialism and anti-colonialism.

The Congress came to power after independence and played an important role in determining the fundamental tenets of India's foreign policy. The main framework of Congress's foreign policy is shaped by its strong adherence to the principle of non-alignment. Highlighting India's pivotal role in the evolution of non-alignment, the Congress [I] viewed: "The non-alignment was born out of the aspiration of achieving national self reliance and delineated precisely the perceptions about the security requirements, within the broad perspective of securing a just and equitable world order."[1] This the Congress opined was the guiding force behind India's independent approach in the tumultuous times of the cold war.

Further analysing the overall performance of India's foreign policy the Congress opined that India was potent enough to comprehend the turbulence in world politics affected by the end of cold war. The Congress [I] has observed: "India took note of the changed world scenario in the 1990s and has evolved meaningful initiative to position the country in such a way that we maintain the continuity of our foreign policy."[2]

The Congress [I] is of the view that end of cold war, has not enfeebled but has enhanced the significance of non-alignment. It stated: "The end of cold war increases rather than reduces the imperatives for fashioning a world order that will secure, the freedom of all States, sovereign equality of all, non-interference in the internal affairs of others, democracy in international relations, peaceful co-existence and opportunities for the full flowering, through mutual co-operation of the potential of the member States and the human family."[3] This is the solemn conviction that has governed the present Indian Governments approach to non-alignment and in this frame of mind Indian prime minister participated in the recent NAM summit in Havana, symbolising India's commitment to uphold the dignity of non-alignment despite criticism from various quarters.

The Congress pleads for reforming the UN. The party is of the opinion that for the complete realisation of the ideals of India's foreign policy, it has to seek a strong and more effective role in the UN. For this the organisation should be strengthened and democratised by giving adequate representation to the third world countries. Regarding nuclear disarmament the party favours the emergence of a nuclear weapons free world. Further, it holds that the question of nuclear disarmament is a global one and it opposes any attempt to regionalise or sub-continentalise the issue.

Regarding SAARC, the Congress [I] recommends the establishment of a non-legislative parliament for South Asia along the lines of European parliament, which can become an effective forum for discussing various issues of common interest in the region. Hence with this, the Congress believes that the association could be strengthened. The party welcomes the progress made by SAARC by setting up South Asian Preferential Trading

Arrangement [SAPTA] and the South Asian Free Trade Area [SAFTA]

The Congress is in favour of an increased South-South co-operation and it believes that India's status of a full-dialogue partner in the Association of South East Asian Nations [ASEAN] will provide greater avenues for an added role for India in world affairs. The Congress [I] holds that in spite of divergences between India and the US on issues such as the CTBT and NPT, the US occupies a prominent position in India's foreign affairs as it is India's largest trading partner. Further, the party holds that there should be a process of constant dialogue with the US on a variety of issues of mutual interest and efforts must be made to institutionalise the dialogue process.

The Congress holds the view that the traditional ties with Russia must be consolidated. As for China, the party views that the major issue in Indo-Chinese relations is the existence of border dispute and the same should be solved with good faith. The party opines that India must take measures to build closer political, economic, commercial, educational and cultural ties with China. On the whole, Congress's views on India's foreign policy is being summed up as follows: "For fifty years the Congress ensured a durable national consensus on foreign policy. This consensus has been of late destroyed. The first task must be to restore the consensus."[4]

## Foreign Policy Position of the Indian National Congress Towards Indo-Pakistan Relations

The traumatic cleavage of the sub-continent was followed by the independence of India and the birth of a new state Pakistan. But the people of the sub-continent achieved their cherished dream of liberation, not before they had suffered a considerable amount of anguish. They had to undergo the agony of partition of the culturally coherent, geographically contiguous, ecologically and economically similar entity, after hundreds of years of organic existence. The division of the sub-continent was expected to solve a political impasse. However, the apportionment of the sub-continent rather than ending increased the magnitude of geo-political economic and anthropological problems.

Immediately after independence, Indian National Congress formed the national Government and the most urgent foreign policy problem it faced was from partition. The creation of Pakistan which was supposed to end communal bellicosities heightened it. Resulting in the new country becoming a hostile neighbour and Indo-Pakistan relations became a major issue in the field of India's foreign policy. Speaking about the implications of India's partition, India's first prime minister Pandit Jawaharlal Nehru said: "The main thing to remember is that we have been suffering in India not only in Bengal but also in other parts and probably in Pakistan also, from a fever, a sickness which did not begin with the partition, but with the partition certainly aggravated."[5]

Though Indo-Pakistan relations have been estranged, the traditional cultural bonds between the people of the two countries have not been dismantled. There exists even after the partition, a deep rooted inter-relation between the citizens of the two countries. But on the political front the intense rivalry never seems to get attenuated. In this context Pandit Nehru viewed: "A large number of people in Pakistan have their friends and relatives here. Similarly, people in India have friends and relatives in Pakistan. When people come over from the other side and meet their old friends they embrace one another. They forget for a moment the new barriers that have sprung up between them and talk of old times with nostalgia."[6]

The Congress has blamed Pakistan of bringing cold war into the contours of South Asia by joining the US sponsored military alliance. The party is of the opinion that due to Pakistan's military nexus with China, the security of South Asia is in jeopardy. In this regard, a former Congress president K. Kamraj Nadar pointed out : "It is unfortunate that our neighbour Pakistan has thought fit to indulge in the game of fishing in troubled waters."[7]

The Congress party holds that the short spell of Lal Bahadur Shastri's leadership of the nation was a defining phase in the history of bilateral relations between India and Pakistan. His abrupt departure proved to be a great loss to the peace making process with Pakistan. The party opined: "The short, yet eventful and memorable stewardship of the nation by Lal Bahadur Shastri, strengthened the sense of self-confidence in Indian masses which, in fact, was instrumental in leading the country to victory against the aggression of Pakistan in 1965."[8]

The party has hailed India's victory against Pakistan in 1971 as a path breaking event in the history of South Asia, for which the towering leadership of Mrs. Indira Gandhi was responsible. The party viewed: "In December 1971, Mrs. Gandhi helped the democratic forces smarting under oppression of the military rulers in East Pakistan to assert themselves, which led to the liberation of Bangladesh as a new nation."[9]

The Congress party holds that Pakistan has violated the basic spirit of Shimla Agreement by indulging in attempts to internationalise the Kashmir issue. In this context, former Congress leader Natwar Singh had stated: "India wanted to have good relations with the neighbouring country. Shimla Agreement was the basis for having good relations but the Government of Pakistan was bent upon internationalising the Kashmir situation."[10]

According to the Congress, Kargil crisis was the result of callousness on the part of the BJP led coalition Government. The party condemned senior leaders of the BJP led ruling establishment that they were a party to a catastrophe, for which their criminal negligence is responsible. The party commented: "The attitude of Shri Vajpayee led to a lack of vigil on our borders. While Shri Vajpayee slept, the invaders were occupying the treacherous heights from Drass to Chorbatla."[11]

In the opinion of the Congress, Indo-Pakistan relations are characterised by extreme uncertainties. The nature of their relations has become so perplexed that attainment of cordiality and maintenance of sound diplomatic links seems to have become hard-boiled. The editorial of the Congress Sandesh described: "If one were to sum up the state of Indo-Pakistan relations, I would do so by recalling the titles of two novels by Charles Dickens, Hard Times but not Great Expectations."[12]

Even after more than six decades of their inception, India and Pakistan have not found any amicable solutions for settling their deep rooted dissonance. Hence the situation becomes dubious. In this regard, former senior Congress leader Natwar Singh believes: "Indo-Pakistan relations are accident prone, so one has to be extra cautious when dealing with this particular diplomatic dynamite."[13]

According to the Congress, an amicable solution to the Indo-Pakistan disputes can be achieved only through a constant process of constructive engagement in bilateral dialogue on all outstanding issues including the vexed issue of Jammu and Kashmir. The dialogue should be carried out within the framework of Shimla agreement. Defining its position the Congress opines: "The Congress is committed to a meaningful bilateral dialogue with Pakistan on all issues including Jammu and Kashmir within the framework of the Shimla agreement of 1972."[14]

The Congress repudiates any third party interference in the process of talks between India and Pakistan. In the party's view: "According to the Shimla agreement no one else can participate in the talks. It has to be just India and Pakistan."[15]

In the ultimate analysis the views of the Congress on Indo-Pakistan relations are being expressed by the All India Congress Committee: "The AICC believes that the people of Pakistan sincerely desire friendly relations with Indian people with whom they share much of the history and culture of this sub-continent. However, the rulers of Pakistan have given a totally negative response and have aggravated the relations between the two countries by sponsoring terrorism in Punjab, Kashmir and in other areas."[16]

An analysis of the views of the Congress on Indo-Pakistan relations reveals the idea of the party indicating a sense of acceptance that partition of the sub-continent was inevitable. But again it also has a sense of nostalgia. As a great party leader like Pandit Nehru recollects the traditional bonds, which exists among the people despite the political wrangles ushered in after the break up of the sub-continent. It has expressed its opinion that Indo-Pakistan relations are a very complex issue and it is a major challenge confronted by the makers of India's foreign policy. A viable solution to this vexed issue can be discovered only through a constant process of bilateral dialogue to be conducted within the framework of the Shimla agreement.

However, it appears that the dynamic nature of Indo-Pakistan relations and the turbulence in world politics vitiates strict adherence to a particular strategy in dealing with this tempestuous issue. Hence, it can be opined that the Shimla Agreement must be given a fresh look. It must also be revitalised in the light of the changed circumstances especially after the structural changes that have occurred in the post-cold war epoch and the new status of India's foreign policy that it has acquired after India crossed the nuclear Rubicon. Lahore declaration may provide a new paradigm, to deal with the transformative nature of India Pakistan relations. The present Congress Government headed by Manmohan Singh seems to have realised this and is attempting to sustain the continuity of India's foreign policy, without disturbing the trend established by the previous regimes.

## Bharatiya Janata Party

Before analysing the approach of the Bharatiya Janata Party, it is pertinent to understand the approach of Bharatiya Jana Sangh, from which it has been carved out. It also owes its ideological links to the Jana Sangh.

## Foreign Policy Position of the Bharatiya Jana Sangh

According to the Bharatiya Jana Sangh, India's foreign policy must be guided by the factor of enlightened self-interest that is the national interest which includes the welfare and progress of the nation. "This concept of enlightened self interest means to the party, recognition of China, recognition of Formosa, recognition of

DalaiLama's émigré Government, liberation of Tibet, joint military pact with Pakistan, and direct association with western block."[17]

The party was in favour of maintaining a harmonious relationship with all the countries and it sought to work for establishing world peace and mutual friendship between India and other countries. It was of the opinion that India's membership of the commonwealth has not been beneficial to India because of the pro-Pakistan predilection depicted in the British policies. The Jana Sangh expressed its unflinching co-operation with the UN and it is in favour of bringing necessary amendments to the UN charter so as to make the organisation potent enough. So that it can become the real representative of the people and function more effectively as an instrument of world peace and co-operation. The party further stated: "It will try to get a permanent seat for Bharath in the Security Council."[18] This was the broad objective of the party.

Jana Sangh vociferously claimed Kashmir issue to be a major bone of contention in India's foreign policy. Apart from this, the party felt that, to baffle the danger posed by India's hostile neighbour China, it should befriend those countries that face a similar threat because they will become India's natural friends. The Jana Sangh opined that India should strengthen its relationship with countries like Japan, Australia, Malaysia, Thailand and Formosa. This will enable India to put up a joint military front to counter the security threats from China. According to the party, a country's position in the realm of international politics depends upon its economic and military strength. "It is the confirmed view of the Jana Sangh that permanent peace is not possible so long as there exist, political slavery, economic exploitation, social discrimination and selfish lust for power."[19]

The party was obsessed by the notion that China and Pakistan are India's natural enemies; hence it noted that India must mould its foreign policy in accordance with the attitude of its neighbours. Its foreign policy must be fashioned as a response to the behaviour of China and Pakistan. Emphasising that defence and foreign policy are closely inter-twined, the party held that India should strengthen its defence in the light of the perils posed by its two hostile neighbours.

The party strongly favoured more budget allocation for defence and it held that India must go for nuclear weapons. According to the Jana Sangh, non-alignment has become extraneous in the light of the hostile character of Sino-Indian relations. Hence, the party felt that India should adhere to an independent foreign policy based on its national interest. It criticised the ruling Congress for not practising the principles of non-alignment in its genuine purport, because the Congress exhibited some proclivity towards a particular block while dealing with some international questions. Hence, the whole concept of non-alignment becomes irrelevant and needs re-examination. M.L. Sondhi viewed : "India can ill afford the kind of rigid and dogmatic world outlook, which has come to be associated with the policy of non-alignment."[20]

Further, Sondhi observed: "Although it is often paraded that it has contributed to the Indian diplomacy, in fact the non-alignment cult has resulted in depriving India flexibility in the choice of means in a rapidly changing world situation."[21] Criticizing the way in which India's foreign policy has been conducted, the Jana Sangh described: "The foreign policy that India had been pursuing all these years, is based on platitudes and slogans."[22] In its approach towards international relations and foreign policy, there appeared a section within the Jana Sangh, having pro-American proclivity. Mohammad Ali Kishore opined : "Jana Sangh also contained a pro-Western group among its ranks, of which chief spokesman is Balraj Madhok he supports almost all the moves of the US."[23]

Thus, an analysis of the views of Jana Sangh towards India's foreign policy indicates that the party presented a radical outlook on the major issues of India's foreign policy. On one hand, its extreme emphasis on Pakistan and China can be seen and on the other, there is a fierce criticism of the principle of non-alignment and an urge for its re-examination. The party also reflects pro-American leanings. Overall the position of the party on India's foreign policy can be summed up in the words of Shyama Prasad Mukerjee, the first president of the party: "Regarding foreign policy our party believes that it should be more realistic, the primary condition being the advancement of the cause of our own country in the maintenance of peace and goodwill in the international sphere."[24]

## Bharatiya Jana Sangh's Approach Towards Indo-Pakistan Relations

The essence of Jana Sangh's approach towards Indo-Pakistan relations lies in its discontentment of the conduct of foreign policy towards Pakistan. It also criticise the negligence of the fundamental issues such as the border dispute, infiltration, and the problem of minorities and Kashmir, by the Governments in power. The party criticised Pakistan for augmenting tension on the border. The Jana Sangh stated: "Indo-Pakistan relations have been strained since the day Pakistan was established as a separate State. In fact, this estrangement is inherent in the circumstances in which Pakistan was born."[25]

The party considered: "Both communist China and Pakistan as India's natural enemies."[26] The Jana Sangh elaborated the idea that the ultimate and permanent solution of the ills of Indo-Pakistan relations is unification of the two countries and the emergence of an integrated India. Defining its position the BJS believed: "The number of people who are beginning to realize that annulment of partition is essential for the well being of the country and for the maintenance of world peace is daily increasing both in Bharat and Pakistan."[27]

The BJS catered to the notion that a peaceful foreign policy aimed at gratifying Pakistan has not resulted in any advantage to India. Hence, the party called for a structural reorientation of India's foreign policy towards it. As Pakistan has always followed a hostile policy towards India, its foreign policy should be made more stringent in order to counter Pakistan's belligerence. The BJS held the opinion: "The policy of appeasement that has so long been followed has not changed the mentality of the leaders of Pakistan on the contrary it has strengthened it. The Jana Sangh is against giving any concessions to Pakistan."[28]

An analysis of the policy position of the Jana Sangh, towards Indo-Pakistan relations, depicts the fact that like all opposition parties it displayed a sense of reprehension and also made capricious suggestions. It believed that the only solution for various problems of Indo-Pakistan relations like the Kashmir issue, problems of minorities and the border disputes is the integration of the two countries and the creation of a united India. This is an ambitious, philosophical and idealistic viewpoint. If we consider the divergent ideological convictions affirmed in India and Pakistan, integration seems to be preposterous.

Jana Sangh's proposal that unification is the solution is credible, but again it is hazardous to unflinchingly adore to the persuasions of Jana Sangh considering the Hindu nationalistic disposition of the party. As aptly pointed by Geet Puri: "In the literature of Indian politics, political parties and party system in India, the Bharatiya Jana Sangh had been described variedly as reactionary, communal, Hindu revivalist, ultra rightist, militant nationalist in its ideological orientation and organisational behaviour."[29]

## Foreign Policy Position of the Bharatiya Janata Party

Foreign policy position of BJP bears in itself, traces of the ideology and principles laid down by its predecessor the Bharatiya Jana Sangh. BJP assigns top priority to national security and the party criticised the former Congress Governments for not giving proper attention to the crucial issues of national security and for attenuating the significance of consensus on foreign policy. Defining its position the party expressed: "The security of the nation is our paramount duty. In fulfillment of this sacred duty we will ensure that the neglect of defence preparedness by the previous Governments shall be corrected."[30]

Like the Jana Sangh the BJP has been critical towards the way in which the principle of non-alignment has been defined and practised by the Congress Government. Hailing the Janata party Government for conducting India's foreign policy purely on the lines of non-alignment, the party calls for a re-evaluation of the principle of non-alignment in the light of changing international situation. The party has underscored the "Need of genuine non-alignment, without making any changes in the basic postulates of our foreign policy."[31]

The party condemned that India's foreign policy is not circumspect of the genuine requirements of our national interest. Senior BJP leader Jaswant Singh remarked: "We are really in search of a foreign policy, an identifiable and an intelligible foreign policy."[32] Jaswant Singh also highlighted the inevitable link between defence and foreign policy: "I, however, mentioned defence and foreign policies, because there is an inbuilt inter-relation. But that inter-relationship is now a great deal wider, much wider in fact. The whole concept of security is much wider concept. That covers not simply of military security, there is an aspect of economic security, there is the aspect of energy security and there is the aspect of food security."[33]

Deploring the hegemony of super powers at the time of cold war the party contended: "We firmly reject the myth that there is any super power exclusivity in the giving of direction to world events."[34] In this regard, the party criticised India's foreign policy in the initial years as the product of cold war politics. senior BJP leader, L. K. Advani considers: "India's foreign policy framework was based primarily on three facts the cold war between USA and USSR, an ensuring relationship with the USSR which suited both the parties and fluctuating relations with the United States, who stood committed to Pakistan, because of the perception that it was a dependable bulwark against the spread of communism."[35]

Acknowledging the mixed impact of the end of cold war, BJP opines: "Curtain has finally been drawn over the cold war which has dominated world for most part of the current century. The new situation is a challenging one, at the same time it is pregnant with several fresh opportunities to enlarge India's role in global affairs."[36]

Greeting the emergence of democracy in the former Soviet Union, the party counseled for the consolidation of India's relations with the post cold war Russia and other republics of the erstwhile

USSR. It stated: "The end of communism and advent of democracy in the Soviet Union are welcome developments. India and Soviet Union have developed and nurtured their friendship and co-operation for nearly four decades. It is in India's interest to continue to develop friendship and co-operation with the Soviet Union as also with the republics."[37]

Regarding the framework of India's foreign policy in the post cold war era, the BJP indicates that "Our diplomacy must be more vigorous and active bilaterally in order to explain our point of view to seek understanding and support on matters of vital interest to us. Economic diplomacy must be integrated with the conventional diplomacy."[38]

Emphasising the significance of good neighbourly relations, the party advocates the building up of concrete relations with India's large neighbour China. The party notes: "We must make vigorous efforts to remove irritants in our relations with our neighbours. We must consciously strive to normalise relations between India and China."[39] The party condemned the prejudicial character of India's foreign policy that had been characterised by Euro-centricism, in view of this the party suggests for the re-orientation of India's foreign policy in order to make it broad based. It thus indicated: "So far India has mainly looked to the West for political, economic, commercial and cultural contacts. It is about time that we turn our attention to the East."[40]

The party is of the opinion that the star of optimism that dawned after the end of cold war has been eclipsed due to unending International conflicts and there has been a re-incarnation of colonialism and imperialism in a new guise. In this regard the party position is: "The end of cold war brings no peace. It was the found hope of the people of India, that the end of cold war would usher in an era of peace, co-operation and the all round development of friendly relations among the nations of the world. This hope has been belied and there is still conflict and tension in many parts of the world."[41] The party notes that the optimistic cord struck by the end of cold war has not been able to galvanise a qualitative change in U.S.'s foreign policy towards India. The party observes: "We note that the US policy towards this region continues to suffer from lack of vision and we find that it disregards India's political and security interests."[42]

Further, the party stated in its election manifesto of 1996: "The BJP will launch a vigorous campaign for a permanent membership for India in the UN Security Council."[43] calling for the democratisation of the UNO, The BJP believes: "We believe that the existing arrangements in the UN are tilted in favour of certain countries to serve their narrow interests. We are committed to the reform of the UN."[44]

Demonstrating the prominent position it attaches to national security, the party announced: "We are committed to establish a national security council to constantly evaluate security, political and economic threats to security and render advice to the Government."[45] It can be noted that the BJP has kept up its words and after the BJP led coalition Government came to power at the centre in 1998, a national security council was established.

Foreign policy position of the BJP in its initial days was entrenched in the framework of the ideology of its predecessor the Jana Sangh. But the position of the party was liberated from the shackles of the principles of Jana Sangh and the approach of the new party witnessed qualitative changes in due course of time. In addition to this its approach also marks a clear departure from its predecessor, when we evaluate its stance on different issues. For instance dissimilar to the Jana Sangh, the BJP has not unequivocally condemned NAM.

## Foreign Policy Position of BJP Towards Indo-Pakistan Relations

The presence of the Pakistan factor in the perception of BJP regarding India's foreign policy and security concerns is omnibus. Since its inception the party has emphasised the significance of relations with Pakistan in determining the contours of India's foreign policy. Stressing the importance of having cordial relations with the neighbours, the party observed: "It has been the party's view that our national interest is best served by creating an environment of peace and harmony in our neighbourhood. But this can only be done on the basis of mutual benefit and co-operation."[46] Following the foot steps of its predecessor, the party considers that Pakistan is one of India's primary enemies. It commented thus: "We have today exceptionally good relations with all our neighbours except the very hostile Pakistan."[47]

BJP is of the opinion that the fundamental question for India is not just improvement of its relations with Pakistan but a stable Pakistan is always in India's own interest. Senior BJP leader and former Prime Minister A. B. Vajpayee explained in the Lok Sabha: "I have already said on the floor of both the houses and I would like to reiterate that a secure and prosperous Pakistan is in India's interest. We must not remain mired in the past and prisoners of old contentions."[48]

The party condemned Pakistan for indulging in a constant search for military solutions to the disputes with India and it opined that there should be an agreement between the two countries upon the non-use of force. It viewed: "The BJP is of the view that Pakistan must not stay rooted in the prejudices of the past. It must abjure from the established pattern of over arming and commenting on India's internal affairs."[49] As regards the U.S. Pakistan nexus, the party had indicated: "despite the end of cold war there continues a pro-Pakistan tilt in the American policy towards the Indian sub-continent."[50] It may be noted here that unlike the Jana Sangh, the party had not reflected a pro-American tilt in its initial days. But after it came to power and India's foreign policy acquired a nuclear dimension, the party began to importune the U.S. administration for receiving recognition for India as a nuclear power.

An analysis of the approach of BJP towards India Pakistan relations has evinced that the genesis of its ideas can be found in the policies and programmes of the Jana Sangh. However as time has progressed, a clear departure is visible. This manifests in the divergent perceptions of the two parties regarding the fundamental nature of the problem in Indo-Pakistan relations and the probable solutions. For instance, the Jana Sangh had stated that the only solution for the ills of Indo-Pakistan relations was the creation of a united India and the annihilation of partition. But BJP leaders have been disparate to this notion. A. B. Vajpayee remarked: "History can be changed but not geography."[51] Thus Jana Sangh's views were idiosyncratic, marked by political eccentricity, unprecedented for the Indian political system.

**Foreign Policy Position of the Janata Party**

In the short stint at the centre, the Janata party attempted to conduct its foreign affairs within the framework of the fundamental principle of India's foreign policy, that is Non-alignment. It viewed that international situation is a dynamic variable and "The primary task of foreign policy is to respond to the challenges as well as opportunities thrown up by it."[52]

The party also believed that a strict adherence to the principle of genuine non-alignment is beneficial for India's national interest. The hostilities of the cold war could be morally and justifiably countered by an unflinching faith in this principle. This position of the Janata party was highlighted by the then foreign minister in the Janata Government, A. B. Vajpayee: "Non-alignment to most people provided the answer to the dilemma between as it were, thesis and antithesis between the containment of communism and the burial of capitalism."[53]

**Indo-Pakistan Relations**

The Janata party believed in a relationship of co-operation and reciprocation with all the neighbours. It assumed that normal relations with Pakistan will be beneficial for India as it engages the national security perception and the scheme of things for India's foreign policy makers. In this regard, the visit of Janata party Government's foreign minister, A. B. Vajpaee to Pakistan indicated the keenness of the Government to normalise its relations with Pakistan. M.S.Rajan points out: "It was very astute on the part of Mr. Vajpayee to have made the gesture of a personal visit to Islamabad and having given personal assurance to Pakistan Government of the continuation of the earlier policy of speedy normalisation of relations."[54]

The Janata party remained in the main stream of national politics only for a short duration. Hence, there is a paucity of literature regarding the policies and programmes of the party, but from whatever is available, it can be summed up that its foreign policy was based upon the twin principles of pursuit of genuine non-alignment and emphasis on cordial relationship with its neighbours, based upon the maxim of mutual benefit.

**Janata Dal**

At the outset, Janata Dal condemned India's foreign policy as week and inefficient to handle international tumult raked up by the end of cold war. The party viewed: At a time of a grave and traumatic international change, India's foreign policy is conceptually paralysed and operationally dormant, amounting to feeble knee-jerk response to earth shaking events leading to taking a back seat in the comity of nations."[55] arguing for the reshaping of India's foreign policy, in the changed global environment, the party believe that India's global role depends upon a strong and vibrant United Nations. The Janata Dal observes: "India should vigorously join the international enterprises to build the world without conflicts and confrontation, making the United Nations, the pivot of regional and international security."[56]

The party expresses a strong conviction regarding the relevance of Non alignment despite the end of cold war. Anyway, it calls for metamorphosising its role into a forum for economic co-operation among the third world countries. The party holds thus: "Non-alignment as an ideology of independence and dignity of the new nations is, at all times, relevant. But it must find its new creative dimension clearly and unmistakably in favour of world peace and co-operation on equal terms."[57]

The Janata Dal holds that India's relations with the US must be based on the principle of equality and mutual benefit. In the election manifesto of 1996, the party made a solemn resolve to strengthen relations with the US without compromising the sovereignty and dignity of the nation. The party is in favour of revitalising India's relations with Russia after the collapse of the USSR and strengthen its relations with Commonwealth countries, Europe and Japan. Further, the party is in favour of greater co-operation among the countries of South Asia and for promoting this, it states that SAARC must be institutionally strengthened. Janata Dal criticized the interference of the US in the affairs of South Asia in the name of maintenance of balance of power.

Further, the party holds that the border dispute with China must be solved at the political level on the basis of equality and mutual benefit. It notes: "The joint boundary commission could be raised to higher political status and joint expert bodies could identify the border with the latest technique of cartography and begin to resolve the border sector to mutual satisfaction."[58]

Finally the Janata Dal criticized that the Governments have forgotten the importance of consensus building process while arriving at crucial policy decisions on issues of national importance, rendering the process of foreign policy making undemocratic. A senior leader of the party and former prime minister I. K. Gujral viewed : "The main point I am trying to say that, consensus is the strength of India, consensus is the strength of the party But I say with a great deal of regret that, even now, I do not see the process of consensus emerging."[59]

Thus an analysis of the foreign policy position of the Janata Dal depicts the point that the fundamental framework of the party's foreign policy rests upon the plank of the principle of non-alignment. The party is in favour of strengthening India's relations with major powers of the world on the basis of the principle of equality and mutual benefit. For instance, an analysis of the party's views on the Sino-Indian relations indicates that the party upholds the principles of Panchasheel for improving the bilateral relations between the two countries. Lastly like all parties, the Janata Dal underlines the significance of consensus in the process of formulation of India's foreign policy.

## Indo-Pakistan Relations in the perception of the Janata Dal

The perception and attitude of Janata Dal regarding India's foreign policy towards Pakistan must be viewed from the prism of the Gujral doctrine, evolved by its senior leader I. K. Gujral which elucidates the significance of India following an accommodative attitude while dealing with its neighbours. In other words Gujral doctrine advocates that since India is a larger, a more developed and powerful country, it has to exhibit magnanimity in giving certain concessions to its smaller and weak neighbours. The party defines its position thus: "India's external relations under the UF Government has been guided by what is known as the Gujral doctrine. Under this doctrine India has strengthened its ties with the neighbours in South Asia on the basis of generosity and non-reciprocity."[60]

The party is of the opinion that SAARC can act as an effective mechanism for strengthening co-operation between India and her neighbours. For this the party feels that the association must be braced through incorporating more provisions in its constitution. So as to include co-operation in the field of trade and fiscal affairs. With respect to India's relations with Pakistan, the party stated that India's policy must aim at : "making it abundantly clear to Pakistan through diplomacy, public relations and adequate security measures, that it cannot seize Kashmir from India and that the low intensity conflict is a double edged policy that can hurt Pakistan equally, if not more."[61]

Janata Dal is of the opinion that the on-going Indo-Pakistan tensions must not be an impediment for the promotion of people to people contact between the two countries. The party favours more people-to-people contact between the two countries. When the party was in power at the centre, it had announced various steps to boost people to people contact. I. K. Gujral remarked in the Lok Sabha: "To promote people to people relations, we have decided to permit Pakistani tourists to visit India in groups."[62]

An examination of the views of Janata Dal on India Pakistan relations demonstrates that the party attempts to visualise it from the perspective of Gujral doctrine. Its views hinge upon the principle of equal treatment to Pakistan as a sovereign nation. But as a bigger country, India must make some concessions to Pakistan considering its smaller geographic, demographic and military strength. As envisaged in the Gujral doctrine and build a peaceful relation with it. Janata Dal's views on Indo-Pakistan relations indicate that the party favoured the conduct of India's relations with Pakistan on the basis of principles of equality and mutual benefit. The party favours normalising of India's relations with Pakistan without recourse to military means. In the ultimate analysis, it appears here that its views on Indo-Pakistan relations resemble to some extent the policy framework of the Janata party.

**Foreign Policy of the Communist Parties**

The Communist parties in India assign top most priority to the issues relating to foreign policy, because their policy is shaped by the international Communist movement. The Communist party of India [CPI] since its beginning holds that imperialism is a major threat to world peace and considers the US as an imperialist country and criticises it as an enemy of world peace. The foreign policy position of the CPI rests upon its support to world peace, non-alignment, disarmament, anti-imperialism, anti-colonialism and friendship with all, specially the socialist countries.

It viewed that at the time of cold war, it was the efforts of Soviet Union which led to the emergence of a situation of détente between the US and the USSR and the CPI sees the changing international situation: "By underlining the activation of new thinking by Gorbachev leadership which brought about fundamental changes in international relations for the better."[63]

But paradoxically, the party condemned the Gorbachev Government for not practicing socialism according to its fundamental principles as a result of which it got perverted, leading to the disintegration of the Soviet Union. The party thus calls for the re-orientation of the principles of Marxism in order to suit Indian conditions. It argued: "We have to integrate our Marxist theory with the specific conditions in India and the legacy and heritage of Indian culture, traditions and social development and to chalk out our own course for democratic and socialist transformation."[64]

CPI is an ardent proponent of creating a world without wars. It criticised US action in the Gulf in 1990 as imperial. It held that due to the hegemonistic politics of US, which it demonstrated by invoking US trade law 301 against India, as a result of which the process of North South Co-operation collapsed. The CPI opines that to retort the US hegemony, international institutions like the UN, NAM and the SAARC must be strengthened. Through these institutions the third world can be galvanised to act as counter balance. In view of this CPI states: "India must uphold its independence, pursue anti-imperialist foreign policy and strive for strengthening the role of the UN in the world affairs and in co-operation with the like minded, wage a consistent struggle for a new international economic order."[65]

The party also reposes confidence upon non-alignment despite the end of cold war, as an instrument of South-South co-operation and through NAM, socio-economic co-operation among the developing countries could be institutionalised. "From this perspective, the NAM can play an important role in working out concerted measures."[66]

The CPI believes that India's relations with China must be re-vitalised. The party opines: "The unfortunate events of 1962 should not be allowed to become a permanent impediment to the restoration of normal Sino-Indian relations and the border dispute should be resolved on the basis of mutually agreed principles."[67]

An analysis of the foreign policy position of the CPI demonstrates that the party has been inconsistent in its approach to some of the issues in India's foreign policy and relations. This can be noticed in its inconsistent attitude towards the USSR. Initially the party supported the policies of the Soviet Union as constructive and credited it by saying that the USSR has played a vital role in bringing world peace at the time of cold war. It further hailed the democratic policies of Gorbachev and said that it was responsible for bringing qualitative changes in the international affairs. But when there was the collapse of the Soviet Union, the party made a U turn and said that Soviet Union collapsed as its socialism was perverted and it had anti-democratic and bureaucratic features.

Further, it can be said here that the party's foreign policy position chiefly hinges upon two significant factors that is its criticism of US as an imperial power and its probable tilt in favour of China. All these tenets of the CPI's foreign policy came to light after the end of cold war. Hence, it seems here that the foreign policy position of the CPI has undergone a structural change after the end of cold war. But this change particularly relates to its ideological predilections and approach towards socialism. Hence, the collapse of the USSR shoved away the party from the USSR and drove it closer to China. Thus the post cold war foreign policy of the CPI can be described as a critique of anti-imperialist designs of the US, the policy of appeasement towards China and unflinching adherence to the policy of non-alignment.

**The Communist Party of India [Marxist]**

In view of the CPI [M], the disintegration of the Soviet Union and the collapse of socialist system in Eastern Europe have shifted the balance of power in favour of the imperial west. The reason for this according to CPI[M] is "The result of accumulation, distortion and revisionist deviation in applying Marxist Leninist principles to building socialism and deformation in Socialist Democracy."[68]

The party has criticised that the US and other imperialist forces are exploiting the international situation which ushered in after the collapse of the socialist system and hence they are trying to establish their own hegemony and impose a world order which is favourable for them. The CPI [M] viewed that the hegemonistic politics of the US was demonstrated at the time of the Gulf war and the UN was impotent to curb the imperialist designs of the US. For this the party blames the former Soviet Union for conniving with the US and supporting the resolution for a military action in the Gulf in 1990. The party has criticised India for co-operating with the Western powers. But the CPI [M] has hailed the role of Cuba which voted against the resolution and China for abstaining from voting.

The CPI [M] opines that the end of cold war brought about a very challenging international situation, because the US has begun attempts for a quixotic perpetuation of its hegemony and revising the world order for its advantage. In this deleterious situation, the CPI [M] holds that pursuance of an anti-imperialist non-aligned foreign policy will facilitate the restoration of world peace. The party believes that India's national interest both security and economic can be protected and India's urge for a prominent role in world politics can be accomplished by strict adherence to the principle of non-alignment.

But the CPI [M] observes that India has denounced the principles of non-alignment and the Government is co-operating with the imperialist forces in their machinations. In view of this the party criticised the Narasimha Rao Government: "Instead of reviewing non-alignment and strengthening South-South co-operation, it sent troops to Somalia in the civil war to subserve the interest of US imperialism."[69]

The Leftist renitence to the July 18 Indo-U.S. civilian nuclear deal may be envisioned from the spectrum of what we have discussed above. the Left parties in India contested the rationality of India's decision to sign the deal, on the axiom that it is a reincarnation of U.S. neo-imperialism masqueraded as wholesome bilateral co-operation, aimed at curbing India's potential as a growing major power.

The CPI [M] favours close and friendly relations with India's neighbours prominently China. The party opines that the strengthening of bilateral relations between the two Asian giants will be favourable in the protection of vital national interests of both the countries. According to the party, India and China together can play a vital role in world politics and preserve world peace by countering imperialist forces. The CPI [M] hailed Chinese stance on Kashmir issue as China held the position that Kashmir issue is purely a bilateral one and it has to be resolved within the framework of Shimla agreement.

The CPI [M] criticises the discriminatory regimes like the CTBT and the NPT and opposes the US pressures mounted upon India to sign these agreements. It criticised Russia for coming under US pressures. The party articulates that the US: "Got Russia to cancel the agreement to sell cryogenic rocket engines to India and imposed sanctions on ISRO."[70]

An overview of the foreign policy position of the CPI [M] demonstrates that unlike the CPI, the party has maintained a definite position on some of the issues concerning India's foreign policy and relations. The CPI which initially supported the democratic reforms launched by the Gorbachev leadership that is the Perestroika and Glasnost, later on criticised the Soviet leadership that it had perverted the ideology of socialism, which brought about the collapse of socialist system in Eastern Europe and Soviet Union. However the CPI [M] right from the beginning had criticised Gorbachev leadership for revising the principles of Marxism and Leninism. The attitude of the CPI indicates that the party suffers from a dilemma of choice between the Chinese communism and the Russian model. But the CPI [M] has had a firm inclination towards China.

Overall it appears that both the parties do not have solid ideological inclinations while approaching the issues of foreign policy.

The two Communist parties have attempted to dilute their ideological proclivities in order to modify their policy positions in order to fashion it within the purview of the fundamental doctrines of India's foreign policy. Hence, both the parties have supported the principle of non-alignment as the most significant principle of India's foreign policy. Above all the approach of both the parties towards India's relations with world's major powers and prominent neighbours are similar.

## Attitude of Left parties on India Pakistan Relations

On Indo-Pakistan relations, the position of the Communist parties is identical, based on their ideological predilections and the framework of the principles of their party. At the outset the CPI views that Kashmir is the dominant issue in Indo-Pakistan relations. The nature and content of the bilateral relations between the two countries is determined by a single issue Kashmir. The party has opined that Pakistan has made all kinds of efforts to solve the Kashmir dispute in its own favour and hence its Government, in liaison with its main intelligence agency ISI, is waging a proxy war against India. These malign endeavours of Pakistan have been nurtured by the neo-conservatives in the U.S. to bolster it's own imperial interests the CPI comments : "Kashmir continues to be a major national political issue with its international dimension [Pakistan waging proxy war through ISI trained militants] and US imperialists are fishing in troubled waters to realise their own evil designs."[71]

The CPI has expressed a deep sense of concern regarding the increasing tensions between India and Pakistan. The party holds that due to the policy of military aggrandisement followed by both the countries on their borders, a war-like situation has developed in the region, threatening the security environment in South Asia. The party further states that this volatile situation has been exploited by the religious fundamentalists on both the sides for their self-centered purposes and this has worsened the situation. So an aura of uncertainty and insecurity prevails in the region. The party contended: "The 18$^{th}$ Congress of Communist party of India expresses grave concern on the continued tension at Indo-Pak border and further deterioration of the relations between the two countries."[72] The CPI also appeals to the democratic and anti-imperialist forces in Pakistan, not to fall a prey to the influence of the US to solve the Kashmir problem. It should be solved bilaterally without the intervention of outsiders.

According to the Communist party of India [Marxist], Indo-Pakistan relation is the most prominent antecedent that has the potency to determine the texture of geo-politics in South Asia. The party holds that a normal healthy and cordial bilateral relation between India and Pakistan is *sine quo non* for preserving peace and security. According to the party, the relations between the two countries are very complex and the complexities tend to have deepened in recent years. The party believes that the problems between the two countries can be amicably solved by constructive bilateral engagement between them. The party underlines: "The key to peace and harmonious developments in South Asia lies in the complex web of India Pakistan relations."[73]

Further, the party holds that the relations between India and Pakistan have worsened because of the blatant interference of Pakistan in the internal affairs of India by attempting to internationalise Kashmir issue. According to the party, the ruling elites in Pakistan have tried to internationalise Kashmir problem by patronising the secessionist movement in Kashmir. They are doing this to divert the attention of their citizens from the discontentment prevailing in Pakistan due to lack of political stability and socio-economic development. The CPI [M] considers: "The relations with Pakistan have worsened. The ruling class of Pakistan is making Kashmir the central point."[74]

The CPI [M] had criticised the then BJP led coalition Government for coming under US pressure while conducting its relations with Pakistan. The party opines that the diplomatic step that was initiated by the Vajpayee led Government during the Lahore process was basically done under US pressure and with an intention to gain political mileage in the domestic politics. The party says: "Under American pressure and its anxiety to overcome international isolation after the Pokhran blasts, Vajpayee agree to go to Lahore for talks in February this year. The exaggerated claims of success of the Lahore bus trip of Vajpayee were made in the hope of making political capital in India."[75]

The examination of the views of the left parties on Indo-Pakistan relations indicates that both the Communist parties have not given adequate priority to the issues pertaining to Indo-Pakistan relations in their policies and programmes. This has happened because the foreign policy position of the Communist parties is concentrated mainly to facilitate their search for an identity in the international communist movement and it is prominently based on their anti-imperialist struggle. Though the views of both the parties on Indo-Pakistan relations differ in content, they are embedded in similar principles and ideological predilections. Both the parties have accepted the inescapable fact that Indo-Pakistan relations constitute one of the most significant factors in determining the geo-politics of South Asia. They have accepted the centrality of Kashmir issue in Indo-Pakistan relations and their views in this regard reflect a tinge of anti-Americanism.

Both the Communist parties have been ardent critiques of American interference in the affairs of Indo-Pakistan relations specially its role in relation to Kashmir issue. The parties have also criticised that some pro-capitalist sections of the ruling elite both in India and Pakistan have facilitated America to exercise its influence over the region. Hence, it can be opined that the foreign policy position of the Communist parties on Indo-Pakistan relations has been a critique of American role in the affairs of Indo-Pakistan relations and condemnation of the anticipated subservience on the part of India to American interests, while evolving policy alternatives to deal with Pakistan.

An overview of the foreign policy position of major Indian political parties points to the existence of a broad consensus among major political parties, on significant issues of India's foreign policy and relations. They seem to have accepted the fundamental principles of India's foreign policy like the non-alignment as the quintessence of India's foreign policy and have not advocated any structural change in these principles. All political parties have broad agreement over the key problems in India's foreign policy and relations.

This means that the views of political parties on major issues of India's foreign policy such as national security, economic security, nuclear disarmament, foreign trade, neo-imperialism and India's relations with major powers of the world like the US, UK and Russia or with prominent neighbours like China and Pakistan are not contradictory.

However, it is worth noting that although the foreign policy positions of major Indian political parties do not differ in nature and content, but a marked difference is perceptible regarding the interpretation of a particular issue. In other words, political parties have unanimity of opinion when it comes to identifying key issues in India's foreign policy and national security, but when they interpret the same issue; they do it in different ways. This leads to divergence in their prescription of policy alternatives. Anyhow, it seems that in India no political party has strong ideological inclinations; except the left which in due course has considerably diluted its ideological predilections; while formulating their foreign policy position. Hence issues rather than ideology are the determining factor of the nature and content of the foreign policy position of Indian political parties.

On Indo-Pakistan relations, sharp divergence among major political parties do not seem to appear. The acceptance of the significance of Indo-Pakistan relations for India's foreign policy is also beyond doubt. There is a consensus among political parties that the belligerent nature of bilateral relations of the two, poses serious security challenges to India. Hence almost all of them tend to counsel for establishing cordial bilateral relations between the two through peaceful means.

However, political parties differ in their interpretation of the nature and causes of Indo-Pakistan conflict. Congress expresses its strong conviction that despite the geo-political separation of the two the cultural cohesion has not been damaged. Hence, Indo-Pakistan disputes are not completely rooted in the partition but find its origin in the political manipulation of the sentiments of the post partition communal holocaust by the anti-democratic fascist wing in Pakistan's ruling establishment which has disturbed the relations between the two countries.

Paradoxically, the BJP believes that Indo-Pakistan conflict is inherent in the fundamental relegio-cultural differences of people of the two countries that got crystallised at the time of partition. The devious way in which the sub-continent was apportioned, bore the germs of Indo-Pakistan conflict. The party indicated that the faultline which was exposed at the time of partition has been fomented through a heterodox political class in the name of safeguarding religion.

Contrary to this, the Communist parties have visualised Indo-Pakistan conflict from the prism of its anti-imperialist leanings. Hence they have alleged America of hegemonistic interference in the politics of the sub-continent that has aggravated divergences between the two countries. Lastly the Janata Dal indicates that as a larger neighbour, India's role in diluting the conflict is greater than that of its smaller neighbour Pakistan. India by virtue of its size and strength, must exhibit magnanimity and give some concessions to its neighbour that may lead to normalisation of their relations.

Ultimately, the perception and attitude of various political parties towards Indo-Pakistan relations, may not have acted as unavoidable determinants to the shaping of India's Pakistan policy because of the presence of inter-party differences and the divergent ways in which they interpret the problem. But their role in articulating public opinion and transmitting people's aspirations to the policy makers cannot be undermined. In addition to this since India has a democratic Government formed by political parties, their role in the process of policy enactment at the Governmental level is definitive. Above all despite the consensus among the political parties being obscure, it has not substantially hampered the efficacy of India's policy responses.

## *References*


1. Indian National Congress *resolution of the AICC Meeting,* New Delhi, 10-11 June 1994, All India Congress Committee publications, New Delhi, 1994, p. 28.
2. Ibid., p. 29.
3. Indian National Congress *resolution of the AICC Meeting,* Surajkund, 27-28 March 1993, AICC publications New Delhi, p. 25.
4. *Election manifesto of the Congress Party,* general elections, 1999, p. 75.
5. Pandit Nehru, *India's Foreign Policy, Selected Speeches,* 1946-1961, Publications Division, Ministry of Information and Broadcasting, Government of India, p. 462.
6. Ibid., p. 465.
7. K. Kamraj Nadar, Presidential address to the AICC Meeting, Bhuvaneshwar, 1964, *Congress Presidential Speeches,* AICC Publication, New Delhi, p. 430.
8. *Text of Resolutions adopted at the 80th Plenary Session of Indian National Congress,* Calcutta, 1997, AICC Publication, New Delhi, p. 13.
9. Ibid., p. 14.
10. Natwar Singh, *Congress Marches Ahead,* 16th May 1993 - 31st December 1995, AICC Publication, New Delhi, p. 143.
11. *Congress Sandesh,* A Monthly Journal of Indian National Congress, 2(1), October 1999, p. 18.
12. Natwar Singh, K., *Congress Sandesh,* June 2001, p. 5.
13. *Congress Sandesh,* Monthly Journal of Indian National Congress, 3(10), June 2001, p.14.
14. *Election Manifesto of Indian National Congress,* general elections 1999, p. 75.
15. *Congress Sandesh,* Monthly Journal of Indian National Congress, 3(11), July 2001, p. 28.
16. Resolution on International Affairs, *Congress Marches Ahead,* March 1-May 5th 1993, p. 146.

17. *The Statesman,* October 22, 1951.
18. S. P., Mukarjee, Inaugural Address in Bharatiya Jana Sangh Election manifesto 1958 cited in Mohamad Ali Kishor, *Jana Sangh and India's Foreign Policy*, Associated Publishers, New Delhi, 1969, p. 31.
19. Election Manifesto of the Bharatiya Jana Sangh, cited in Mohamad Ali Kishor, Supra, No. 18, p. 32.
20. M. L., Sondhi, Jan-Deep a Souvenir brought on the occasion of the 14th Annual Session of Bharatiya Jana Sangh , Calicut, December 1967, p. 47.
21. Ibid., p. 47.
22. Balraj, Madhok, *What BJS Stands for,* Ahmedabad Junior Chamber, Ahmedabad, 1967, p. 46.
23. Mohammad Ali Kishor, Supra, No. 18, p. 36.
24. S.P.Mukarjee, cited in Mohammad Ali Kishor, Supra, No. 18, p. 36.
25. Mohammad Ali Kishor, Supra, No. 18, p. 141.
26. Deendayal Upadhya, Jana Sangh, *Seminar,* 89, January 1967, p.36.
27. Mohammad Ali Kishor, Supra, No. 18, p. 142.
28. Ibid., p. 142.
29. Geeth, Puri, *Bharatiya Jana Sangh Organisation, Ideology,* Sterling Publications, New Delhi, 1980, p. 5.
30. *National Democratic Alliance, Election Manifesto,* General Elections, 1999, BJP secretariat, New Delhi, p. 1.
31. BJP Resolutions, Adopted at the National Executive Meeting held at New Delhi on September 5, 1980, *Foreign Policy Resolutions and Statements, 1980-99,* BJP secretariat, New Delhi, 1999, pp. 3-4.
32. Jaswanth Singh, *Lok Sabha Debates* 3rd Session, 11th Lok Sabha, 11 Series, VI, Lok Sabha Secretariat, New Delhi, December 4, 1996, pp. 290-291.
33. Ibid., pp. 290-291.
34. BJP resolution adopted at the National Executive meeting held at Cochin on April 23, 1981, *Foreign Policy Resolutions and Statements 1980-1999,* Supra No. 31 p. 6.
35. The BJP: *Presidential address* by L. K. Advani, National Council

Session, 18-20 June, 1993, The BJP secretariat, New Delhi, 1993, p. 17.

36. BJP *Election manifesto,* general elections 1991. p. 25.

37. *BJP resolution adopted at the National Executive meeting* held at Thiruvanthapuram on September 30, 1991, BJP secretariat New Delhi.

38. Ibid., p. 31.

39. Ibid., p. 30.

40. Ibid., pp. 32-33.

41. *BJP resolution adopted at the National Executive meeting* held at Vadodara, on June 9, 1994, Foreign Policy Resolutions and Statements 1980-1999, Supra No.31, p. 51.

42. *Foreign affairs section of the BJP election manifesto,* general election 1996.

43. Ibid..

44. *Foreign Affairs Section of the BJP's Election Manifesto,* general elections 1998.

45. Ibid.

46. *Foreign Policy Resolutions and Statements 1980-1999,* Supra No.31, p. 1.

47. Ibid., p. 1.

48. Atal Bihari Vajpayee *Lok Sabha Debates,* Twelfth Lok Sabha, Twelfth Series, 2(9), June 8, 1998, Lok Sabha Secretariat, New Delhi, p. 478.

49. *BJP resolution adopted at the National Executive meeting* held at New Delhi on April 13-14, 1981, BJP secretariat, New Delhi.

50. *BJP resolution adopted at the National Executive meeting* held at Vadodara, Supra No.41, p. 51.

51. N.M., Ghatate, [ed.], *Decisive Days of Atal Bihari Vajpayee,* Shipra Publications, New Delhi, 1999, p. 215.

52. Atal Behari Vajpayee, India and the Changing International Order, in K.P. Mishra [ed.], *Janata's Foreign Policy*, Vikas Publishers, New Delhi, 1979, p. 1.

53. Ibid., p. 2.

54. M.S., Rajan, *India's Foreign Policy: Problems and Perspectives,* in, Ibid, p. 22.
55. The Janata Dal: *Resolution adopted by the National Executive meeting* held in New Delhi, on 7-8 September, 1991, Janata Dal Publications New Delhi, .
56. The National Front *Election Manifesto* of 1991, National Front Publication, New Delhi, 1991, p. 39.
57. The Janata Dal: *Resolution of National Executive meeting* held in New Delhi, Supra No.55, p. 10.
58. Ibid., p. 12.
59. I.K. Gujral, *Lok Sabha Debates* [English version], 29th May 1998, Second Session, Twelfth Lok Sabha, Twelfth Series, 2 (3), Lo Sabha Secretariat, New Delhi, 1998, p. 347.
60. Janata Dal *Election manifesto,* Lok Sabha Elections, 1998, p. 3.
61. The Janata Dal: *Resolution of National Executive,* New Delhi, Supra No.55. pp. 10-11.
62. I.K. Gujral, *Lok Sabha Debates,* Eleventh Lok Sabha, Eleventh Series, 11(21), March 20, 1997, Lok Sabha Secretariat, New Delhi, p. 229.
63. *Development in the Soviet Union and Eastern Europe,* Communist Party Publication, New Delhi, 1991, p. 13.
64. Ibid., p. 21.
65. The *CPI Election Manifesto,* general elections 1991, p. 8.
66. The CPI: *Political Resolution adopted by 16th Congress of the Communist Party of India,* Delhi, 7-11 October, 1995, New D e l h i , CPI Publication, 1995, p. 7.
67. *New Age,* 25 December 1991, p. 7.
68. The CPI [M]: *Political Resolution adopted by the 14th Party Congress,* Madras, 3-9 January 1992, CPI [M] Publication, New Delhi, 1992, p.4.
69. The CPI [M]: *Political Resolution adopted by the 15th party Congress* held at Chandigarh on 3-8 April 1995, CPI [M] Publication, New Delhi, 1995, p.30.
70. Ibid., p. 30.

71. Communist Party of India: *Resolution adopted at 16th National Congress,* Supra No.66 p. 84.

72. Communist Party of India, *Resolution adopted at 18th National Congress* held at Thiruvanthapuram, March 26-31, 2002, p. 178.

73. Communist Party of India [Marxist], *Document of the Resolution adopted at 17th All India Congress* of the Party, Hyderabad, 2002, p. 26.

74. Communist Party of India [Marxist], *Document of the Resolution adopted at 15th All India Congress,* Supra No. 69, pp. 31-32.

75. *13+4 months of BJP Misrule Pokhran to Kargil,* No. 5, CPI [M] Publications, New Delhi, 1999, pp. 6-7.

# Chapter 6

# The Kashmir Issue

One of the most significant aspects of international politics is that nation States tend to assert their sovereignty even through military aggrandizement. This tendency of nation States may lead to military conflicts. The primary component of a country's national interest is the protection of its territorial integrity. In process of doing this, countries may entangle themselves in disputes because of their equal and common claim over a particular territory. Another dimension of such a conflict can be witnessed when two countries clash with each other on the issue of defining their boundaries.

Finally irredentism, the claims of a country for a particular region, which is now under the jurisdiction of its neighbour may lead to conflicts among nations. In this context, the examples of Israel Palestine, India China and India Pakistan can be cited as nations enmeshed in chronic bilateral territorial disputes. Kashmir presents itself as one of the most glaring illustrations of exasperated territorial disputes denoting Pakistan's irredentist claims.

Kashmir issue is a major determinant of the nature of the entire gamut of bilateral relations between India and Pakistan. The defence and foreign policies of both countries are conditioned by their positions and claims over the territory of Kashmir. All other issues between the two are convoluted in the Kashmir issue. The resolution of major issues between the two countries such as terrorism and nuclear arms race depends upon the peaceful settlement of Kashmir issue: "It will not be an over simplification to state that the lack of normal healthy and stable Indo-Pakistan relations is also due to unresolved Kashmir issue."[1]

American role acted as a catalyst in accentuating decadence in Kashmir by engulfing Pakistan into its game of cold war politics which bolstered the megalomaniacal fantasies of a section of Pakistan's anti-democratic elite. On its part, the role of India in making Kashmir issue perplexed is equivalent to that of Pakistan. In the 1980s, the Indian Government showed a sense of indisposition to curb infiltration into Kashmir valley.

Zia was able to take advantage of the situation and financed and developed Madrasas which became centers for nurturing the extremist Islamic fundamentalist ideology among young Muslims who later on carried out subversive activities in Kashmir. As a result of this Kashmiri Pandits were driven out. All this led to the psychological infection of Kashmiri youth with jihadi concept. The emergence of terrorism in Kashmir paved a way for the appearance of *quasi fascist* religious fundamentalist forces which have depraved the system of liberal democratic politics in Kashmir.

The result is men with guns have taken the centre stage and the territory has become a battle ground for quenching the thirst for political domination nurtured by some sections of the ruling class on both sides of the border. Sushant Sareen viewed : "Politically through religious symbolism and rhetoric used by the Pakistani establishment has led to the rise of Islamic radicalism within the country. The proliferation of arms coupled with military training to the Mujahidins fighting in Kashmir and the politicization of jihad has raised only the specter of an armed Islamic take over. The social impact of privatization of jehad in Kashmir has been devastating."[2] The valley has also become a hot bed of intrigues, and a platform for promoting vested interests.

The Kashmir issue has the dubious distinction of being the most debated subject in both India and Pakistan. It has captivated the discourses of the mass media, academia and also the public sentiment and is a major concern of foreign policy makers and defence strategists on both sides of the border. All this is primarily due to the high stakes of both the countries on the territory. "For India and Pakistan, Kashmir is a concept not a territory. The significance of Kashmir lies in a combination of factors. The most important among them arises from historical, traditional and cultural identity."[3]

## The Present Geo-political Status of Kashmir

Before knowing various dimensions of Kashmir issue from a historical perspective, it is pertinent to understand the current geo-political position of the region of Jammu and Kashmir. The total area of the region is 2.22 lakh sq. kms. Out of this, approximately 35 per cent that is about 78.000 sq. kms., is under the illegal occupation of Pakistan. Pakistan was able to capture the region and establish a Government under its indirect control at the time of tribal intrusions into Kashmir in October 1947. It can be observed: "Only the Gilgit area called the Northern area is directly ruled by Pakistan".[4]

"Pakistan has handed over about 2 per cent of the region that is about 5,000 sq. kms. to China which in turn has constructed a strategic highway linking Sinkiang province".[5] Besides, China has already forcefully occupied about 17% of the region that is about 35,000 sq. kms. "Hence, the total area upon which India has sovereign authority is nearly 46 per cent that is about 1.01 lakh sq. kms."[6]

This area is divided into three parts - firstly Jammu covers an area of about 26%, Kashmir covers an area of 16% and Ladakh covers an area of about 58%. The demographic set up of Jammu and Kashmir shows a disproportionate ratio in terms of the size of the three different parts. The population of the three regions is – 45% in Jammu, 53% in Kashmir and 2% in Ladakh, which is not on par with the size of their areas. This is due to the topography of the region. For instance, in spite of Ladakh having about 58% of the territory, its population is only 2% of the total population of Jammu and Kashmir. This is due to the still unconquered difficult terrains of the region.

At the North East of the region lies Chinese border, to its further North Khazakistan, and to its North West Afghanistan. The Karakoram highway runs through the region and Saichin glacier holds a very strategic position Thus from the geo-political perspective Jammu and Kashmir is located in a very strategic position. The control of the region by any power will give it an upper hand over its neighbours and it will be in a position of preponderance politically, economically and geographically. The strategic relevance of the region was sighted by the foresighted British statesman at the time of India's independence. Colonel Ravi Nanda points out: "The British at that point of time felt that the Soviet Union may try to extend itself to the unsettled Sinkiang. Lord Ismay was aware of this British strategic interest in this area. Therefore, a loyal Government in the strategic North West had to have Jammu and Kashmir as an integral part."[7]

## The Genesis of Kashmir Problem

The Kashmir issue is complex and multi-dimensional, having intricate and diverse factors that have made it as a seemingly intractable problem. Sumantra Bose maintains: "In its contemporary incarnation the Kashmir conflict has both exogenous and endogenous sources which reinforce each other in a particularly intractable combination."[8]

The roots of Kashmir issue can be traced to the fermentation of separatist tendency, which took deep roots in the Indian society at the time of British rule in the 19th century. The Muslim minority which had the legacy of ruling over Hindu majority for a long time, found its political domination challenged due to the entry and subsequent ascent of the British to the citadels of political power in India.

Commensurate to this, there occurred a qualitative change in the socio-political status of the Hindus and Muslims at the time of imperial rule. The progressive Hindus took advantage of English education, but the orthodox Muslims showed a sense of inhibition. Ultimately the socio-political status of the Hindus was increased which was not the case with Muslims. Here lie the seeds of political separatism between Hindus and Muslims that became so intractable that partition became inevitable.

But partition did not emerge as a solution for the problems of the sub-continent; on the contrary, it became a source for endless new problems. The most prominent being the dispute over Kashmir. "The original conflict about Kashmir was never inevitable. It became an acute problem soon after the independence of India and Pakistan because, many partition problems remained unsolved."[9]

Thus partition resulted in Kashmir becoming a platform for using the threat of Hindu domination to promote the interest of Pakistan that resulted in the emergence of what can be termed as a communally motivated political psychopathology. The successful exploitation of this Political paranoia by the military junta of Pakistan enabled it to perpetuate its political jingoism and justified the prevention of the emergence of a secular Parliamentary democratic system of governance.

At the outset, legally India was declared an independent State and Pakistan was created as a new State by the independence of India Act of 1947, enacted by the British parliament. This Act was formulated beyond the framework of the Government of India Act of 1935, spelling out a provision for sovereign princely States of the erstwhile Indian colony, that, "they had the choice of joining any of the two nations by signing an instrument of accession."[10]

On the basis of this, most of the princely States joined India and Pakistan. But some States preferred to remain independent. Kashmiri king decided to declare Kashmir as an independent

State and signed a stand still agreement with Pakistan. The location of Kashmir locked in between two large neighbours created several economic and political problems for that State. But still the king persisted with his decision, despite persuasions from both India and Pakistan to join either of the two. It is worth noting: "In India before the independence, the Congress and the Muslim League were seriously concerned regarding the future status of Jammu and Kashmir."[11] The Muslim League had the pretension that as the region was a Muslim majority area; the territory should be under Pakistan. On the other hand, the Congress had the notion that as the National Conference professed a secular ideology the State would definitely accede to India. But it happened the other way round. The State did not join either of the two.

### The Tribal Intrusion and Kashmir's Accession

The British divided Indian sub-continent on demographic basis, so Muslim majority areas were partitioned to create Pakistan and the Hindu majority areas remained in India. The accession of the independent princely States was left to the decision of the rulers of their States. But even the princely States acceded to the nascent countries on the principles of geographical contiguity and demographic similarity. On this ground, the Muslim majority princely States acceded to Pakistan and the Hindu majority princely States joined India: "Kashmir posed a particular problem, it had a Hindu king Hari Singh and a Muslim majority population abutted both the future India and future Pakistan."[12]

But the skepticisms of Indian and Pakistani leaders were ended quiet against their expectations when Raja Hari Singh of Jammu and Kashmir expressed his decision to remain independent. Here lies the springs of Pakistani irredentism and its leaders began to claim: "Kashmir issue as an unfinished task of partition."[13] The anti-democratic fascist wing within the Pakistani ruling establishment was anticipating an opportunity to fulfill this unfinished task. "Meanwhile, during the first week of October

1947, a tribal rebellion broke out in the Poonch region of the South-western reaches of Kashmir."[14]

Pakistan saw in this an opportunity to cherish its unfulfilled dream and finessed a regular military operation in the guise of a tribal revolt. The royal army of Raja Hari Singh was not capable of countering the tribal attack backed by the Pakistani military. Hence, he approached the Indian Government for help. "Lord Mountbatten told Nehru that unless the Maharaja of Kashmir signs the instrument of accession, the Government of India had no authority to send troops which would be construed as invasion of a foreign territory."[15]

Hence, the Indian Government began negotiations with the king for persuading him to accede to the Indian union. "The Kashmir ruler had then hesitated to sign the instrument of accession to India. But when the hordes of militants from Pakistan invaded Kashmir, he signed it on October 27, 1947."[16]

In this way, the State attained its present status of being a part of Indian union and was accepted by the people of Jammu&Kashmir. With this, the calculations of Indian National Congress proved to be correct. Before independence, it had expressed the hope that in the wake of a choice between India and Pakistan, the popular organisation the National Conference with its secular credentials would express its consent in favour of India. "The point that the accession of Jammu and Kashmir to India was a desperate decision stood neutralised, because the most representative political organisation of the people of Kashmir, the National Conference endorsed the accession of Jammu and Kashmir to India under the leadership of Sheikh Abdullah".[17]

Thus after Maharaja Hari Singh signed the instrument of accession with the Government at New Delhi, Kashmir became an integral part of Indian union and now the Government was empowered to send its army for counter action against the tribal intrusions. Tantamount to this, the Pakistani Government stepped up its operations. Soon a pitched battle began between the

Indian and Pakistani defence forces. Initially the Indian troops faced difficulties due to the inhuman topographic conditions and rough weather. It was only in November 1947, that the Indian forces were able to launch a major offensive against Pakistan. Though the Indian army succeeded in arresting the onslaught and pressing the intruders away from Srinagar, the tribal forces were able to hold on to nearly one third of Kashmir valley. They declared it as independent Kashmir or Azad Kashmir. The Pakistani army assisted the Azad Kashmir forces to set up an interim Government at Muzafarabad.

In due course of the battle, the Indian forces had to face logistical difficulties, such as lack of adequate supplies, lack of training in high altitude warfare and lack of equipment. Due to this, the counter operation was enfeebled. Taking advantage of Indian troubles, the Azad Kashmir forces were able to push Indian military to a literal retreat. In the beginning of 1948, the Indian military launched fresh attacks, which brought greater Pakistani engagement in the war. "As the fighting continued, the Indian leadership came to the ineluctable conclusion that the war would drag on indefinitely unless Pakistani support for an involvement with the insurgents ended."[18]

Meanwhile, the security threats to Kashmir was averted by Indian military action, but "As the danger to Kashmir subsided, the question of its future constitutional status came up for discussion at various levels."[19] Hence intense discussions began regarding the mode of ascertaining the wishes of people about the status of the State. "Mountbatten suggested a plebiscite to be held under a neutral agency or the UN, but only after law and order had been restored."[20]

Now the Indian leadership confronted a precarious situation because, the valley had not yet been cleared of the intruders and they did not want to increase the magnitude of the conflict. Faced with this predicament Pandit Nehru decided to take the Kashmir question to the UN. He did it even when the intruders had not been driven out of the valley completely. This made the

Kashmir issue more complex. And it was internationalised. Even if the Indian Government had conducted the plebiscite as promised, the Kashmiris would have voted in favour of joining India. This was bound to happen because of the mass support which Sheikh Abdullah enjoyed among the Kashmiris. Sheikh who adhered to a secular ideology and who did not enjoy Jinna's favour, preferred to remain in India.

The bilateral relations between India and Pakistan became a subservient of the Kashmir problem. The peaceful relations between the two countries depend upon the amicable solution of the Kashmir issue. Subsequent analysis of the history of the Kashmir issue will show how the conflict has evolved as a deciding variable in the geo-politics of South Asia. For India and Pakistan, Kashmir does not symbolise a geographical entity, but epitomises their national identities. Robert G. Wirsing writes: "The Kashmir dispute is obviously not just about positioning a line on a map. Even at its outset in 1947, it held meanings that went well beyond that and since then it has helped to shape and in turn being shaped practically all aspects of relationship between India and Pakistan."[21]

## UN and Kashmir Issue

After the Indian Government referred the Kashmir question to the UN, the latter made an attempt to bring an amicable solution to the dispute: "The United Nation's Security Council was formally called upon to deal with the Kashmir situation on January 1st 1948, when the Indian representative at the United Nations transmitted to the president of the council a complaint from the Government of India. India anxious to proceed according to the principles and aims of the United Nation's charter, reported the situation under article 35 of the charter."[22]

India defended its case by stating that it responded to the appeal for assistance by Jammu and Kashmir Government on two important grounds. Firstly, India could not let a friendly neighbouring State to determine its domestic affairs and foreign relations under duress. Secondly, as the State had acceded to Indian union, it was the responsibility of the Indian Government to protect the States security and territorial integrity.

The Indian case was presented to the Security Council by its representative, Gopala Swamy Ayyangar. He stated that India had approached the UN with deep regret and it had a request for an immediate action by the supranational body. The Indian contention was that the people of Kashmir would be given full independence to determine their destiny after the entire valley had been cleared of intruders. Pakistan also presented a counter complaint to the Security Council denying all the Indian allegations.

Its contention was that India had indulged in the acts of persecution of Muslims and it followed a genocidal policy against its Muslim minority. It stated that India has never accepted partition and showed a sense of hostility against Pakistan in implementation of the partition agreements. Pakistan argued that Indian Government had conspired against the people of Kashmir by annexing their State by force. So Pakistan coloured the issue in its own way in order to divert the attention of the international community.

The first action of the Security Council with regard to the Kashmir issue was its dispatch of telegrams to the Governments of both India and Pakistan by the secretary general of the UN on behalf of the president of the Security Council. It stated that both the parties must refrain from acts that displayed bellicosity which may be considered as violation of the UN principles. In that case, the council would take a necessary disciplinary action.

Both the countries accepted the move. Then the Security Council moved a resolution on 17th January 1948, calling both the parties to take desirable measures to improve the situation, Even this resolution was accepted unconditionally by both the parties. The resolution made a provision for setting up of a commission to deal with the matter. This was known as United

Nations Commission for India and Pakistan [UNCIP]. The commission consisted of three members one from India, another from Pakistan and the third from a choice made by both of them.

On April 21 1948, the Security Council passed another resolution, in which the strength of the UNCIP was increased from 3 to 5. The resolution called upon Pakistan to take concrete measures to clear the valley of raiders. It also called upon India to reduce the size of its security forces to a minimum level required for maintenance of law and order. Further to represent the spectrum of the States population, the resolution proposed the creation of a coalition for Jammu and Kashmir. Lastly, it stated that a plebiscite should be conducted to ascertain the wishes of the people of Kashmir. This resolution became a reference for all the future actions of the Security Council.

On 3rd June, the council passed another resolution directing the UNCIP to visit the area under dispute and study the situation in the framework of the complaint lodged by Pakistan on 15th January 1948. The UNCIP visited the sub-continent in June 1948 under the leadership of Josef Korbel. The commission came up with its report which was submitted to both the Governments on August 13, 1948. The report called for an immediate cease-fire and end of their hostilities. It also recommended the conducting of a plebiscite to ascertain the wishes of people of Kashmir under the auspices of the UN, after law and order is restored in the State.

Pakistan's abstinence of non acceptance of the resolution sprung out of its rigid position on the status of Azad Kashmir. This compelled the commission to conclude that "The commission observes with regret that, the Government of Pakistan had been unable to accept the resolution without attaching certain conditions beyond the compass of this resolution. Thereby making impossible an immediate cease-fire and the beginning of fruitful negotiations between the two

Governments and the commission to bring about a peaceful and final settlement of the situation."[23]

In view of this the commission expressed skepticism of an early and amicable solution of the entanglement. It gave an opinion that the partition of the State might be a better option to solve the problem, thus ended the first phase of the UNCIP efforts to unravel the Kashmir conundrum. However the commission could not get much success.

Further, on 5th January 1949, the commission came up with a supplementary resolution reaffirming its earlier proposals about a plebiscite under the UN auspices with the plebiscite administrator appointed by the secretary general of the UN. According to the resolution, the plebiscite would be conducted only after the two conflicting parties agree upon a cease-fire and end all hostilities.

Here it can be noted that before the resolution was formally published on January 5th 1949, it was submitted to the Governments of India and Pakistan in December and subsequently in the same month both Governments expressed approbation. As a result, a ceasefire was affected on 1st January 1949, and the troops of India and Pakistan were ordered to halt their advance and maintain status quo.

The UN delineated the cease-fire line, separating the Azad Kashmir from the Indian side. This delineation before clearing the valley of its intruders became a great fumble, as it legitimised the occupation of that part of the State by the pro-Pakistan Azad Kashmir forces. The boundary between the two countries was called the cease-fire line and it was designated as the line of control after the Shimla agreement. This was a reaffirmation of the notion of the permanence of cease-fire line and legitimised of Pak occupied Kashmir outside the purview of Indian state of Jammu and Kashmir.

After this, the United Nations Commission for India and Pakistan [UNCIP] was dissolved and the UN decided to take the route of one man mediation and Owen Dixon and Frank

Graham were appointed as UN mediators successively. But the deadlock on demilitarisation and the failure to conduct a plebiscite due to the persistent armed conflict, led to the mediation efforts of the UN to become a futile exercise. Even the bilateral negotiations from 1951 to 1956 did not yield any results and it came to a grinding halt, when Nehru stated that he was ready for a partition of Kashmir on the cease-fire line.

In 1957 India-Pakistan problem again became a multi-lateral issue when again it was introduced in the Security Council. This time Frank Graham was deputed to the sub-continent proposing a resolution which was tautological as it contained nothing more new than his earlier proposals. The resolution was rejected by India and the role of UN in the resolution of the Kashmir issue practically came to an end.

Apart from this, the military alliance of Pakistan with the U.S., brought a fault line between the ideological predilections of the two countries as India adhered to the principle of non-alignment in the conduct of its foreign policy. Pakistan's entry into the military block dragged Kashmir dispute into the vortex of cold war and the prospects of a plebiscite defaced and India was retrograded from an active involvement in finding new avenues to resolve the dispute.

In addition to this, general Ayub Khan's wrecking of democratic mechanism and the military takeover in Pakistan in 1958, made India harden its position on bilateral negotiations. Nehru stated that he was not willing to talk to general Ayub Khan as he was undemocratic, "It was in this background that India initiated the democratic process in Jammu and Kashmir and at the same time rejected any role for the UN or any external party in resolving the dispute."[24]

But all this did not dampen the spirit of Pakistani ruling elite and its irredentist claims over Kashmir did not relapse. They still vociferously argued that Kashmir remained as an unfinished agenda of partition and harboured the notion that the existence of Pakistan with a distinct identity as an Islamic State in South Asia requires Kashmir to be included in their nation. On its side, India despite all this did not give attention to the demands of Pakistan and remained firm on its stance to strengthen its grip on Kashmir in order to demonstrate its secular credentials.

Both nations remained stranded on these anti-thetical positions which again led them to a bump point and another war in 1965. So an insight into the first phase of the history of Kashmir dispute shows how an internal dispute of India became a bilateral conflict between India and Pakistan and later developed into a major international issue after the matter was taken to the UN. The overview of the events of this period also depicts a series of follies committed by the Indian Government in handling Kashmir issue, leading to a debate over the fundamental nature of the conflict that whether it is a domestic problem of India or is it an international crisis involving its neighbour Pakistan.

## Article 370 and Special Status for Kashmir

The Indian Government was not able to conduct plebiscite in Kashmir as promised. The practical difficulty which the Indian Government faced in complying with its promise was the unremitting armed conflict between India and Pakistan in the territory, ending of which was a necessary pre-condition for holding a plebiscite. Despite the cease-fire declared by India and Pakistan, in accordance with the UN guidelines, hostilities did not end. In such a predicament, Indian Government began the process of uniting Kashmir into the Indian union and tighten its grip upon the State by providing a special status for Kashmir wide Article 370 of the Indian constitution.

The Article provides that the State shall have full internal autonomy and the central Government will have the powers to legislate and execute only in areas such as defence, external affairs and communications. A separate constituent assembly was formed in 1950 and it drafted a separate constitution for Kashmir. The State was given large scale of autonomy compared to the other Indian States. "In 1974 the six point Kashmir accord between Sheikh Abdullah and Indira Gandhi gave permanence to Article 370 of the Indian constitution."[25]

But as the time has rolled by and the crisis in Kashmir intensified due to greater Pakistani engagement, the people of Kashmir have been the ultimate sufferers. The counter insurgency operations of the Indian security forces and the gross human rights violations that they have committed compelled the people of Kashmir to develop a feeling of alienation and disillusionment resulting in a boisterous claim for autonomy. In the meantime Pakistan expressed a deep sense of indignation over the way in which India carried out the process of absorbing Kashmir within its union.

## The War of 1965

Since then Pakistan has been persistently asserting that Kashmir is the central issue in its relations with India. The sentiment of the Pakistani ruling elite which existed at the time and which have persisted even up till now can be summed up in the words of the present president of Pakistan General Pervez Musharraf: "Let us be pragmatic. Let us learn to accept harsh facts that Kashmir is at the center stage of Indo-Pak relations and has to be settled in an equitable and honourable way acceptable to India, Pakistan and Kashmiris."[26]

This provoked Pakistan to consider its own ways to settle the issue in its favour. It led them to resort to a forceful means to capture Kashmir, leading to the first Kashmir war. Although the UN intervention had been successful in bringing an end to the war, its failure to bring an amicable solution to the problem led to the second war in 1965.

At this juncture, the military regime of Pakistan realized that the difficulty of a smooth and an early settlement of Kashmir issue became complicated. Apart from this, the politicization of Kashmir issue in the United Nations led India to lose its interest in implementing the UN resolutions and it gradually began the process of integrating the State into the Indian union. In fact it tightened its grips on the territory by strengthening its military hold. This frustrated Pakistan.

On its part India, exhibited an equal determination to hold on to Kashmir, even by resorting to the use of the military force. The Indian leaders had warned Pakistan right from the beginning about India's commitment to protect the territorial integrity of Kashmir. "For example as early as 1952, prime minister Nehru in a new year address had categorically stated that if Pakistan invades Kashmir, we will not only meet them in Kashmir, but it will be a full scale war between India and Pakistan."[27]

"The 1965 war of India and Pakistan had been fought around the Kashmir issue. Ayub Khan had thought that India's hold over Kashmir, had been weakened in the wake of wide spread disturbances in the State after the holy hair at Hazratbal in Srinagar had been mysteriously stolen and equally mysteriously restored."[28] By virtue of this event, Pakistan forged a flawed inference that there is a pro-Pakistan wave in the region.

In addition to its serious endeavours to resolve the Kashmir dispute peacefully, there was: "India's readiness to refer Pakistani claims over Jammu and Kashmir to the international court of justice in 1953. Pakistan turned it down hoping that India after the feat against China was amenable to pressure and that they could get a better deal."[29] These antecedents magnetised the Pakistani military and political elites to launch its operation Gibraltar, the strategy to attack Kashmir, initially by infiltrating men into the territory with an intention to foment an internal rebellion and then taking advantage of the volatility for a full scale war.

It may be noted here that "Just before the 1965 war, the Pakistani Government had infiltrated forces into the Indian zone to promote insurgency, the response from locals was both direct and negative, and no uprising took place."[30] After this, Pakistan launched a full scale attack in Kashmir by sending regular forces.

The Indian response was gallant and its army crossed the cease-fire line and met Pakistani forces. There occurred a fierce battle in which Indian troops gained an upper hand and they were able to move into Lahore sector, ultimately threatening to capture Lahore.

The armed hostilities were ended when the Security Council passed a resolution calling upon both the countries to end the war which both the parties agreed. The post-war settlement between India and Pakistan was reached at the summit meeting between Indian Prime Minister Lal Bahadur Shastri and the Pakistani president Ayub Khan in Tashkent, which was arranged with the assistance of Soviet mediation. The two parties signed an agreement which stated that one of the parties will withdraw to the position prior to the start of the war. The two signatories agreed to observe a cease-fire on the cease-fire line and solemnly resolved to settle their disputes peacefully.

**The Bangladesh Crisis and Shimla Accord**

The 1971 war between India and Pakistan was not fought around Kashmir issue. The main reason for the war was India's involvement in the secessionist struggle of East Pakistan. But Pakistan extended the war to the Western front, bringing Kashmir into the scene. However, in a decisive battle, India was able to defeat Pakistan on both fronts and the war resulted in the creation of Bangladesh.

The post war negotiations held at Shimla between Indira Gandhi and Z.A. Bhutto was a curtain raiser to the most significant event relating to the Kashmir conflict. This was concerning the Cease fire line which was agreed by the two parties to be renamed as the Line of Control and both leaders pledged to strive to affirm its status as the permanent international border. This aspect of Shimla accord has brought long-standing ramifications upon the nature of Kashmir dispute.

But Zulfikar Ali Bhutto's successors did not maintain the sanctity of the LOC, inspite of Indian admonitions. The Pakistani military has made several attempts to revise the LOC for its advantage. Its first major attempt was in 1987 under operation Brastacks, engineered By Zia-Ul-Haq. Its next significant attempt resulted in Kargil crisis, leading to a fourth war.

Pakistan has been boisterously stating that it will not accept the LOC as the international border. General Pervez Musharraf in an interview to the Washington Post said: "Islamabad will not accept the Line of Control, dividing Kashmir between India and Pakistan as the international border. Accepting the LOC as the international border or granting some sort of autonomy to Kashmir would not solve the problem. If the line of control were to be the border, what have we fought two wars for."[31] This is a blatant violation of the Shimla accord.

## The Low Intensity Conflict or Pakistan's Proxy War in Kashmir

"The term low intensity conflict LIC, covers a large spectrum of hostile activities, without the armed forces of the adversaries coming into direct confrontation."[32] Kashmir exemplifies an outstanding case in modern history, which has been a victim of a low intensity conflict or a proxy war sponsored by Pakistan. After, all the direct ways - both military and diplomatic - to settle Kashmir issue failed, Pakistan decided to attain its ends through machinations.

It began to foment indigenous terrorist activities in the 1980s in Kashmir by taking advantage of the disturbed situation. Pakistan began to promote terrorism in the name of Islam, Madarasas were funded to preach jihad and Terrorist training camps were setup with the help of the ISI. This led to the mushrooming of myriad of indigenous and foreign terrorist groups in Kashmir and the State became a hub of intense militant activities.

The Pakistani designs of a proxy war in Kashmir were based on the paradigm of creation of fear and disillusionment among the people of Kashmir. This was done through a proxy war entrenched in the principles of extremist Islamic fundamentalism masqueraded as jihad or holy war. The idea was to encourage subversive activities backed up by false propaganda in order to create a sense of disenchantment and hatred towards Indian Government.

The key intention was to engage Indian military in a chronic low intensity war in order to sap its resources and demoralise its troops so that they become vulnerable to any future offensive. By fomenting subversive activities, not only in Kashmir but in various parts of India, Pakistan wanted to destabilise India from within, that is bleed India by a thousand cuts. To execute its sinister designs, Pakistan created a cabal consisting of its key intelligence agency ISI and several militant groups operating from within and outside Kashmir. Pakistan made a heavy funding and also received resources from foreign countries to nourish its Madrasas and terrorist training camps.

The Inter Services Intelligence agency of Pakistan has played a pivotal role in promoting terrorism in Kashmir. "Indeed, Kashmir was the only area in India in the mid-1980s, where Islamic revivalism had taken a radical political stance and the slogans of Islamic State have been publicly raised and have been received with growing popularity."[33]

Thus through a proxy war, Pakistan wanted to project Kashmir as an ignition point and internationalise it. It has ensured that the costs of the low intensity conflicts do not become extravagant and there shall be no transgression of the perceived limits of India's tolerance. The bottlenecks in the domestic, political and economic scenario which led to the disillusionment of the Kashmiris acted as a catalyst in accentuating the terrorist movement. Pakistan claims: "Only to provide moral and diplomatic support"[34], to the rightful aspirations of the Kashmiris for self determination.

Thus, for nearly two decades the valley has become an epicenter of fierce terrorist activities, characterised by an intense battle between the militants and Indian security forces. In the wake of this the human rights situation has dropped to a nadir. Chronic terrorist violence and the oppressive counter-terrorist operations have amounted to serious human rights violation of the Kashmiris.

The Islamic outfits have attempted to change the demographic and cultural complexion of Kashmir, through orchestrated propaganda and violent oppression they have resorted to the Islamisation of Kashmir, tarnishing its indigenous culture. "As the insurgency in Kashmir valley gained momentum, the acts of sabotage increased in terms of frequency and intensity. The security forces and the paramilitary troops reacted violently, often at the expense of innocent civilians. The abuse of human rights by the security forces has been a persistent and serious cause of concern. Stories have emerged of torture, rape and indiscriminate killing."[35]

## Nuclearisation of India-Pakistan and the Kashmir Issue

India Pakistan relations assumed a perilous posture after their nuclearisation in 1998. This has added a new dimension to the intricate Kashmir issue. The territory which is a pivotal element in the ambit of their bilateral relations has emerged as the hub of intense military activities. The emergence of India and Pakistan as declared nuclear States, has led to the further deterioration in the security situation of Kashmir, forcing Western analysts to call it as a nuclear flash point in South Asia.

The conventional arms race which germinated after Pakistan joined the military alliance sponsored by the USA in 1953 seems to have metamorphosised into a nuclear arms race after both the countries conducted nuclear tests in 1998. The nuclear deterrence that emerged after these tests has proved to be counter-productive for the Kashmir issue. Instead of leading to a reduction of tension, dangers of a nuclear war now looms large over entire South Asia.

## The All-Parties' Hurriyat Conference and the Kashmir Issue

"The all-parties' Hurriyat Conference is an alliance of 34 Kashmiri Muslim parties and organization fighting for Kashmir's freedom from Indian control."[36] It claims to be the sole representative of the people of Kashmir. Its leaders assert that they should be made a third party during the negotiations conducted over Kashmir issue.

The APHC is a conglomeration, consisting of diverse groups which do not have a common ideology or *modus operandi,* but have a goal for the liberation of Kashmir. Its objectives find an expression in the words of Amanullah Khan, JKLF activist, an extremist militant outfit which is a part of the Hurriyat conference: "My point of view is that it is in the best interest of not only Kashmiris but of India and Pakistan, that the Kashmir issue is solved in a way without hurting the national egos of India and Pakistan, without harming the national interests of India and Pakistan, without harming the national ideologies of India and Pakistan."[37]

The All-parties' Hurriyat conference follows a double-edged policy. On the one hand, it wants to involve in the process of pacific means like dialogue for the resolution of Kashmir issue. But on the other hand, it does not abandon violent methods of exerting pressure on Indian Government. Apart from this, despite the APHC's claims of being the representative of the people of Kashmir, it has a definite pro-Pakistan tilt: "The leaders of All-parties' Hurriyat conference can be described as being slaves of a situation, whose controls are being operated from somewhere else. That is why they have to rush to Pakistani high commission now and then to seek guidance."[38]

The Indian Government has constantly engaged in a dialogue with Hurriyats and urged its extremist wing to abandon violence and participate in the democratic process. But it can be said that its endeavour to "hold talks with Hurriyat are flawed, because the latter is not the representative of Kashmiri people."[39]

## Kargil Crisis and Kashmir Issue

The Pakistani intrusion in Kargil sector of Indian side of Kashmir was another attempt by Pakistan to shift the balance of power in Kashmir in its own favour and revise the posture of LOC which has been a *de facto* border between the two since 1949. In short Pakistan's fundamental motive behind its action in Kargil was to make some territorial gains. The most astounding aspect of Kargil crisis was that the Pakistani military took a unilateral decision to intrude into the sector superceding its political masters. Hence this came as a surprise to India because, after Lahore declaration, India had made a flawed inference that its relation with Pakistans was harmonious.

The top Indian elite were under the impression that the declared nuclear status of India and Pakistan may bridle any intention of Pakistan to think of military adventure in Kashmir. But their perceptions proved faulty due to Pakistani perfidy. Although India was able to achieve a military and diplomatic victory in the Kargil crisis, it brought deep seated ramifications on Kashmir issue. The epicenter of conflict over Kashmir shifted from the valley to Ladakh region and the framework of bilateralism which the Shimla accord had provided was pushed into shambles as Pakistan attempted to internationalise Kashmir issue.

## Cease-fire in Kashmir of December 2000

"The unilateral cease-fire is the most significant initiative taken by the Indian Government since 1996 for restoring peace in Jammu and Kashmir."[40] Even after the fiasco of Lahore and Pakistani perfidy in Kargil, the former Indian Prime Minister A. B. Vajpayee took a candid step by announcing a unilateral cease-fire in Kashmir. It was declared that India would desist from armed hostilities for the holy month of Ramzan in the year 2000 A D, despite threats from militant outfits to thwart the initiative. It was also extended for another month. It was felt: "The second extension of what is loosely called the cease-fire in Jammu and Kashmir, is both an opportunity and challenge for Pakistan. For

India, on the other hand, it is an article of faith after all the so-called Kashmir problem has never been sought by this country to be solved by military means."[41]

Anyhow, inspite of this noble gesture, there was no significant increase in the pace of the dialogue process. Hence, under the duress of terrorist violence, the Indian Government had to withdraw its cease-fire initiative. This exhibits the complex nature of the Kashmir problem.

**The Agra Summit**

"The Vajpayee Government which had taken a tough stand against the Government of General Musharraf for over throwing the democratically elected regime in Pakistan and for earlier masterminding the Kargil operations against India and had refused to talk to the leadership suddenly made a U turn and took the dramatic step of inviting General Musharraf to India for summit talks."[42] In July 2001 the summit meeting between the Indian prime minister, Vajpayee and the Pakistani president General Musharraf was conducted at the historic city of Agra. But the summit which began with a high note and media hype, proved to be a inconclusive. There was no unanimity over the core issue in the agenda for talks. Pakistan claimed that Kashmir was the core issue and India asserted that terrorism was the central issue. Hence, lack of unanimity resulted in the failure of the summit.

The most glaring aspect of the Agra summit is that the complexity of Kashmir issue again came to light and the summit depicted the fact that without Kashmir being the core issue, there will be no chances of a peace deal between India and Pakistan. In this context, it would be worth noting the views of Yasin Malik a JKLF activist on Kashmir issue. "Kashmir is not a territorial dispute. It is about the future and survival of people of Jammu and Kashmir."[43]

## September 11 Terrorist Attacks on America

The terrorist attacks on the U.S. on 11 September 2001, brought about grave ramifications on global affairs. Kashmir which has become a hub of terrorist activities has not remained reticent. "The Kashmir dispute has changed since September 11. As a result of the campaign against terrorism, militant groups fighting there will come under sharp pressure to cull their ranks of Binladen sympathisers and Arab and Afghan fighters."[44]

The terrorist activities have witnessed a sharp decline after America initiated a global campaign against the menace. Pakistan also came under US pressure to take concrete steps to curb the growth of Islamic fundamentalism in its territory. But as a paradox, terrorism has not ceased from creating havoc not only in Kashmir but in many other parts of India. The terrorist attacks on Jammu and Kashmir assembly house on October 1, 2001 bears testimony to this.

On December 13, 2001, the perceived bounds of terrorist activities crossed the limits when the heart of Indian democracy, the Parliament house complex was targeted. Due to this, Indo-Pakistan relations dropped to a nadir and Kashmir was exposed to a danger of another deadly war. There was heavy troop mobilisation on both sides of the border. The Indian Government declared that it will not engage with Pakistan for any dialogue, until terrorism ends. Contrary to this Pakistan's president General Musharraf, in two of his famous addresses to the nation, gave a solemn assurance that he would affect coagulated moves to flush out Pakistani soil from all terrorist structures. "Despite President Pervez Musharraf's professed seriousness about de-escalating of violence, the ground realities in terror-torn Jammu and Kashmir seem hardly to change."[45]

The most outstanding impact of September 11 terrorist attacks are that the world began to recognize the gravity of the problem in Kashmir. Hence, India was able to exert pressure on Pakistan through coercive diplomacy. But in spite of the war-like situation, India and Pakistan were unable to arrive at any feasible deal resulting in an impasse. In the second half of 2002, India and Pakistan pulled back their troops and the war clouds which loomed over the sub-continent were cleared off.

As a quid pro quo, the then prime minister A.B. Vajpayee announced in April 2003 that India was ready for a dialogue with Pakistan on all outstanding issues including Jammu&Kashmir. Commensurate to this several diplomatic initiatives and confidence building measures were also declared. Prominent among them was the proposal to start a bus service from Sri Nagar to Muzafferabad, the capital of Pak occupid Kashmir. This demonstrated Indian inclination for recognising the present status of Pak occupid Kashmir and legitimise the LOC. This phenomenon gets credence after there was a change of guard at the center and the UPA Government came to power. Exhibiting the continuity in India's foreign policy, it did not deviate from the course followed by the previous Government and launched the bus service, indicating its acceptance to that policy. This also shows how India's foreign policy is conditioned on the basis of a national consensus.

Thus an analysis of the Kashmir conflict illustrates the way in which it has determined the course of bilateral relations between India and Pakistan. In the four wars that have been fought between the two and the various agreements that they have reached, Kashmir issue has featured prominently. The issue seems to have acquired the dubious distinction of being the core issue in the ambit of their bilateral relations; the fiasco of Agra on the single point agenda of Kashmir and Pakistani misadventure in Kargil, despite the consciousness of a situation of weaponised deterrence which is now evolving in the region, provides credence to this phenomenon.

With terrorist violence seeming endless, Kashmir issue affirms itself to be the most significant problem confronted by India's foreign policy makers. The recent terrorist attacks on Mumbai and the subsequent destabilization of the bilateral relations of India and Pakistan and Manmohan Singh's repeated assertions of India's stance that their can be no comprehensive dialogue with Pakistan until cross-border terrorism ends. All indicate to the inevitable interface between the Kashmir issue and cross border terrorism. As long as this inter-connection persists, Kashmir will continue to kindle, keeping it at the highest point in Indo-Pakistan equations.

## *References*


1. K. Subramanyan, *The Hindu,* 5th November 2003.
2. Sushant, Sareen, *National Herald,* 28th February 1999.
3. Madhavee, Inamdar, *Indian Express,* 25th February 1997.
4. K. Subramanyan, Supra, No. 1.
5. Hari Jaising, *Kashmir A Tale of Shame,* UBS Publication, New Delhi, 1996, p. 21.
6. *Ibid.,* p.21.
7. Colonel Ravi Nanda, *Kashmir and Indo-Pak Relations,* Lancer's Books, New Delhi, 2001, p. 25.
8. Sumantra, Bose, Kashmir Sources of Conflict, Dimensions of Peace, *Economic and Political Weekly,* 34(13), March 27, 1999, p. 762.
9. Lars Blinkernberg, *India-Pakistan The History of Unsolved Conflicts,* Vol. II, Odence University Press, Odence, 2001, p. 46.
10. J.N., Dixit, *India Pakistan in War and Peace,* India Today Group, New Delhi, 2002, p. 309.
11. Alstare, Lamb, *Kashmir, The Birth of a Unending India-Pakistan Tensions Since 1947,* Oxford University Press, New Delhi, 2002, p. 15.
12. *Ibid.,* p.15.
13. J. N. Dixit, Supra, No. 10, p. 309.
14. Prem Shankar, Jha, *Kashmir 1947, Reveal Versions of History,* Oxford University Press, New Delhi, 1996, p. 16.

15. Govind, Talwalkar, Nehru, Kashmir and UN, *The Radical Humanist,* 63 (10), 5th January 2000, p. 5.

16. Instrument of Accession of Jammu and Kashmir, *Indian Recorder,* December 4-10, 1993, p. 14.

17. J.N., Dixit, Supra, No. 10, p. 308.

18. G.C., Raju, Thomas, *Indian Defence Policy*, Princeton University Press, Princeton, 1986, p. 18.

19. Govind, Talwalkar, Supra, No. 15, p. 5.

20. Colonel Ravi Nanda, Supra, No.7, p. 25.

21. Robert G. Wirshing, *India-Pakistan and the Kashmir Dispute; on Regional Conflict and its Resolutions,* by Rupa and Company, New Delhi, 1995, p. 9.

22. Sisir, Gupta, *Kashmir A Study in India-Pakistan Relations,* Asia Publishers, Bombay, 1966, pp. 141 and 142.

23. *Ibid.,* p.185.

24. J. N. Dixit, Supra, No. 10, p. 309.

25. Aswini, K. Ray, From Autonomy to Self Determination, The Politics of East Pakistan and Kashmir, *Economic and Political Weekly,* 36 (49), December 8, 2001, p. 4542.

26. Pervez, Musharraf, *The Times of India,* 15th March 2004.

27. Nehru as cited in T.V.Paul, *Asymmetric Conflicts : War Initiation by Weaker Powers,* Cambridge University Press, Cambridge, 1995, p. 109.

28. Kalim, Bahadur, *Democracy in Pakistan Crises and Conflicts,* Har Anand Publications, New Delhi, 1998, p. 249.

29. T. Sreedhar, *Deccan Herald,* 24th May 2003.

30. Alexander, Evans, Kashmir: The Past Ten Years, *Asian Affairs,* 30(86), February 1999, p. 23.

31. Ajoy, Ghosh, *Indo-Pak Conflict Threat to South Asian Security,* Reference Press, New Delhi, 2003, p. 152.

32. Afsir Karim, The Conflict in Kashmir, *Seminar* 479, July 1999, p. 20.

33. ISI Finger in Kashmir, US Report, *Indian Recorder,* December 4-10, 1993, p.15.

34. Jonab Blank, Kashmir: Fundamentalism Takes Root, *Foreign Affairs,* 78(6), November/December 1999, p.43.

35. A.S., Hilali, Kashmir: Emerging Nuclear Threat in South Asia Perspectives, *The Central European Review of International Affairs,* 16 Summer 2001, p. 43.

36. Yoginder Sikand, Changing Course of Kashmiri Struggle From National Liberation to Islamist Jihad, *Economic and Political Weekly,* 36(3), January 20-26, 2001 p. 220.

37. Interview with JKLF activist Amannullah Khan, *Mainstream,* 38(30), July 15, 2000, p. 17.

38. Shyam, Kaul, Hurriyat Rides a Tiger, *National Herald*, 31 May 2000.

39. Nilofar Suhrawardy, *The Hindu,* 24 May 2000.

40. Muchkund, Dubey, For a Broad-based Dialogue with the Kashmiri People, *Mainstream*, 29(20), February 24, 2001, p.6.

41. G.S., Bhargava, Kashmir Cease-fire, General Musharraf's Stakes, *Mainstream,* 39(9), February 17, 2001, p. 23.

42. P.S., Jayaramu, Vajpayee Musharraf Summit, Room for Cautious Optimism, *Mainstream*, 29(29), July 7, 2001, p. 6.

43. Yasin Malik, *Times of India,* 19th March 2004.

44. Alexander Evans, Talibanising Kashmir, *The World Today,* 57(12), December 2001, p. 14.

45. Praveen Swami, Machination in Kashmir, *Frontline,* February 15, 2002, p. 17.

Chapter 7

# Approach of Political Parties Towards The Kashmir Issue

Political parties as vital links between citizens and the Government are in a decisive position to determine India's policy responses to the Kashmir issue. diluting of the one party dominant system and India's entry into a multi party system, has provided a broader platform for a comprehensive debate over the fundamental reasons for the emergence of the Kashmir conundrum and discuss the remedial action to be adopted to deal with this exasperated problem.

For long India's foreign policy has been characterised by a consensus and this consensus also reflects in India's policy response to the Kashmir problem which is marked by a unanimous admission among Indian political parties of the critical dimension of the Kashmir issue in their perception and evaluation of Indo-Pakistan relations. Their role in exploring feasible solutions to deal with the issue gets accented, inspite of their differences in the interpretation of the nature of the problem. In the light of this, an analysis of the attitude of Indian political parties towards the Kashmir issue would be significant.

## The Indian National Congress

The Congress, which came to power immediately after independence, has witnessed the Kashmir dispute right from its genesis as a ruling party. It has persistently stated that Kashmir is an integral part of India and it is purely India's internal issue and rejects any attempts to internationalise the matter.

The party contends that democratic process of dialogue should be the base for its solution. It also acknowledges the necessity for involving the Kashmiris in the process. In this regard the Congress states: "The Congress reiterates that Jammu and Kashmir is an integral and inalienable part of the Union of India."[1]

Congress holds that Pakistan's hostile and irredentist attitude has been solely responsible for the emergence of Kashmir imbroglio. According to Pandit Nehru: "It is impossible to escape the conclusion that the raids on Kashmir were carefully planned and well organised by Pakistani authorities, with the deliberate object of seizing the State by force and then declaring its accession to Pakistan."[2]

Congress party reposed its trust upon the U.N. for attaining a solution for the Kashmir entanglement. This conviction pressed the then Congress Government to refer the Matter to the U.N. Defending this action Nehru observed: "Our making a reference on this issue to the Security Council of United Nations, was an act of faith, because we believe in the progressive realisation of a world order and a world Government."[3]

The Congress is in favour of holding a dialogue with various groups in Jammu and Kashmir which represent a wide spectrum of the State's population. The party is committed to promote the socio-economic development of Jammu and Kashmir and it believes that grant of adequate regional autonomy to the State would facilitate the accomplishment of this task. The party maintains: "The Congress is open to dialogue and discussion with any group within the framework of the constitution. The issue of regional autonomy will be given serious and critical consideration."[4]

The party expresses its strong adherence to the spirit of Article 370 that grants special status to Jammu and Kashmir. It is of the opinion that the wills and aspirations of Kashmiris can be protected by respecting the constitutional provisions laid down in Article 370. Hence, in its 1999 election manifesto the party stated: "The Congress stands committed to respecting Article 370 in letter and spirit."[5]

The Congress criticises the Opposition parties for raising an abstruse antipathy to Article 370. It apprehends that by raising the issue of Article 370, the opposition seeks to gain a political mileage and misguide the people of Kashmir. The Congress expresses its solemn resolve to bring a pacific settlement to Kashmir issue. In doing this, the party states that it will not accede to any populist demands for the revision or abrogation of any section of the Article. A senior leader of the party Vayalar Ravi stated: "I have really failed to understand what the leaders of the opposition want to gain by raising this issue. I could draw a conclusion that they are only trying to drive away the people of Kashmir, frighten them and make them feel that they are not a part of this nation."[6]

The Congress is of the view that Kashmir's internal and external troubles began immediately after the non-Congress Governments came to power at the centre. The party holds that non-responsive and improper governance of the non-Congress Governments at the centre are responsible for outbreak of militancy and subsequent alienation of Kashmiris. The Congress maintains: "Militancy in Jammu and Kashmir, was the first tragic consequence of the Congress remitting office at the centre after the elections of November 1989."[7]

Criticising BJP led Government's policy on Kashmir, the party as an opposition argued: "The situation in this crucial State has gone from bad to worse, because the BJP-led Government at the centre lacks any strategy; political or security-related-to work towards a comprehensive settlement with the different shades of opinion in the polity and the different reasons of the State to facilitate the participation of all in democratic and peaceful manner in the politics and governance for the State."[8]

Speaking in the Lok Sabha the Congress leader Jaipal Reddy said: "There is a limit to endurance of the people, and there is a limit to patience of the opposition parties. No Government in the history of India has been such a dismal failure on the law and order front."[9] However, the Congress praised some steps adopted by the then BJP Government for the resolution of Kashmir imbroglio.

For instance, the party hailed the Government's step of declaring a unilateral cease-fire in Jammu&Kashmir, but condemned the unscrupulous methods of policy implementation on the part of the Government that led the terrorists to pirate this initiative. Present Prime Minister Manmohan Singh had stated in the Rajya Sabha: "We had expressed the view that we hoped this time the Government had taken all possible precautions that the militants would not take undue advantage of this cease-fire. The killing of innocent truck drivers is a most ghastly incident. It once again, reinforces the plea that the Government while it negotiates, while it offers not to take the initiative in counter-insurgency measures, should never weaken its guards against these elements."[10]

The Congress led UPA coalition Government came to power in 2004 at the centre. It expressed its commitment to maintain the continuity of the peace process in order to find concrete solutions to Kashmir issue. "In a departure from the past, New Delhi submitted to Islamabad a set of Kashmir specific proposals on transport links, trade, cultural, co-operation, tourism, environment and people to people contacts."[11] The successful launching of the Srinagar-Muzafferabad bus service by the Manmohan Singh administration epitomises this and also indicates the party's pledge to maintain continuity in Kashmir policy. This endeavour on the part of UPA Government has renewed hopes of people of both countries for revitalising peace in the State.

A review of the policy position of Congress on the issue of Kashmir brings us to the conclusion that the policies are self-contradictory. Since the transpiration of the problem, various policies adopted by the Congress led-Governments were marked by incongruities. The Congress party claims that the whole of Jammu and Kashmir is an integral part of Indian Union. But since the beginning Congress Governments have not followed their professed policies. If it is the declared stand of the Congress party that it is committed for a united Kashmir, then what led the Indira Government to accept the cease-fire line as the *de facto* border and declare it as the line of control in the Shimla agreement?

The acceptance of the line of control implies that India is not pressing for Pakistani vacation from the so-called Azad Kashmir which constitutes nearly one third of the princely State of Jammu&Kashmir. If this was the case, the party could have inhibited from propagating that the whole of Jammu and Kashmir is an integral part of Indian Union. But it did not do so. The party's popular agenda of claiming the entire State as an integral part of the Indian union obscures its position on Azad Kashmir and amounts to the violation of Shimla agreement that had accorded legitimacy to the cease-fire line as the *de facto* border. Above all, the Narasimha Rao Government aggravated the divergent perception by bringing a resolution in the parliament for re-integration of Pak Occupied Kashmir in to the State of Jammu & Kashmir. Hence, it seems here that the Congress has not evolved a comprehensive and consistent policy towards Kashmir. Hari Jai Singh opines: "The Congress leaders have not shown that they know how to deal with the situation. Merely changing governors or political brokers do not constitute a policy or a strategy. We did not have policy in 1947, we do not have one today."[12]

**Bharatiya Janata Party**

Before analysing the views of BJP on Kashmir issue, it is pertinent to examine the views of its predecessor Bharatiya Jana Sangh. The party believed that whole of Jammu&Kashmir is an integral part of Indian union and Pakistan is attempting to grab it by force. It held that, as legally Kashmir is an integral part of India, it should not be internationalised and should not be considered as an issue. In this regard Jana Sangh leader Premnath Dogra remarked: "Jana Sangh looks upon Jammu and Kashmir as an integral part of Bharat as any other great part of our country."[13]

The Jana Sangh stoutly opposed conducting of plebiscite in Kashmir and dubbed it as illogical. The party viewed: "The Jana Sangh feels that all talks of plebiscite are irrelevant and altogether unconstitutional."[14] The party stood for the abrogation of Article 370. It articulated: "Article 370 which is today simply an anachronism should be deleted from the constitution of India and this would enable the people of Jammu and Kashmir to be one with the nation."[15]

The views of Bharatiya Jana Sangh on the issue of Kashmir are radical and revolutionary. Its position is a reflection of its view that roots of Kashmir dispute may be found in the partition of sub-continent and it considers that the re-unification of India and Pakistan is an ultimate solution. This is unfeasible and the suggestion denotes political eccentricity. It reckoned that the provision of Article 370 was a compensatory provision and it was merely a conciliatory policy. But in admiration of the domestic tumult in Kashmir and the international turmoil at that time, the provision seemed sagacious. Lastly, counseling for the re-integration of the parts of erstwhile princely State of Jammu and Kashmir under the occupation of Pakistan leads to the belief that the party is advocating military solutions to deal with the problem.

The BJP also has expressed very radical views on the issue of Kashmir, tantamount to those of its predecessor, the Jana Sangh. As an opposition it condemned the Indian Government for not devising a prudent policy towards Kashmir. It viewed that the policies of Congress Governments did not give proper heed to the internal problems, pertaining to the socio-economic and political development of the State. The BJP holds: "the absence of political far-sightedness and clarity of national objectives has resulted in our nation continuing to have to pay a price even fifty years after Jammu and Kashmir became a part of the republic."[16]

BJP emphasises that the whole of Jammu&Kashmir, even those under Pakistani occupation as an integral part of the Indian union. It contended: "The BJP affirms unequivocally India's sovereignty over the whole of Jammu and Kashmir including the areas under foreign occupation."[17] Condemning Pakistan for perpetrating terrorism, BJP urged the Government of India to perspicuously tell Pakistan that the latter should stop patronising terrorism in Kashmir. Its leader Madan Lal Khurana emphasised: "The Government should clearly tell Pakistan that it should stop encouraging terrorism in Jammu and Kashmir. A lot of bloodshed has taken place there."[18]

Criticising the Government for its failure to evolve prudent steps for arresting Pakistani sponsored terrorism; it stated that espousal of uncompromising methods are required to deal with the problem. The party believes: "Half a decade of Pakistani terrorism perpetrated in Kashmir should be enough to convince the Government of India that it cannot continue to shirk its responsibility to the country. If Pakistan does not end its aid and abatement to the terrorists soon, India will have to decide on what steps to take against Pakistan to curb its nefarious activities in Jammu and Kashmir."[19]

The party as an opposition denounced the Government's policies on Kashmir as symbols of improvisation and maintained that it led to the internationalisation of the dispute. L.K. Advani opined: "In the absence of thought, there is no stability in our policy *ad hocism* has caused great harm to our national interest. The internationalising of Kashmir has already been cited."[20]

Opposing the grant of autonomy to Jammu and Kashmir, the party viewed that if greater autonomy is granted to the State, it will lead to the strengthening of anti-democratic fundamentalist forces in the State which is detrimental to the vital security interests of the nation. It will also create more socio-political instability in the State. The party is critical of those groups who argue in favour of greater autonomy. The BJP leader Jagmohan viewed: "Today, the whole continent is being swept by the waves of fundamentalism. New philosophy, new ideology has come and the people's minds have changed, their attitudes have changed. How do you meet the onslaught of those forces."[21]

Defending the idea of abrogating Article 370, the party explained that due to domestic disturbances in the State and international pressure from across the border, status of Kashmir is in question. Hence, the only solution to stabilise its status and protect India's national security is the abrogation of Article 370. In the 1991 election manifesto the party articulated: "The Pakistani-inspired violence against Hindus has caused those Kashmiris to become refugees in their own land. The BJP will end all uncertainties about the future status of the State by deleting Article 370 of the constitution."[22]

BJP is in favour of reclaiming Pak-occupied Kashmir in order to bring a permanent solution to the entanglement and to solve the internal problems of the State. The party asserted: "the BJP realises the magnitude of the challenge and dedicates itself to the task of not only solving the internal problems of the State but also reclaiming the portion of our territory which has been illegally held by Pakistan for nearly five decades."[23]

This statement eulogises BJP's recognition of the gravity of the Kashmir problem. The party regards the problem as one that has encapsulated the entire national psyche. L.K. Advani argues: "No single issue claims greater attention of the national minds today than the situation in Jammu and Kashmir. Pakistan's decade-long proxy war against India has now entered a deadly new phase."[24]

Contesting against politicisation of the Kashmir problem, L.K. Advani criticised the partisan approach to the problem as myopic. In view of this he stated in the Lok Sabha: "this problem should not be viewed from the party angle. We should unitedly think over this problem and find a solution to it. The issue is related to the entire country."[25]

The views of the BJP on the issue of Kashmir reflects the fact that the party has taken a very radical outlook towards the problem. It appears that the Hindu nationalist foundations of the party and its parental links with the right wing Jana Sangh might have lured the party to give such revolutionary views. The party's idea that the permanent solution to the problem lies in reclaiming the areas of Kashmir which is under the occupation of Pakistan, resembles to those of the Jana Sangh. Such suggestions are capricious and drive us to conclude that the party is counseling for military action in Kashmir.

Considering the fragile framework of the Kashmiri society and the geo-political antecedents in which the region is embedded, it would be deleterious to tamper with delicate sensitivities. In other words it would be better as Pandit Nehru put it; not to open the Pandora's Box; and it would be judicious on the part of our strategists to maintain status quo. Even the BJP leaders are coming to terms with the situation and they have moderated their position on the issue of reclaiming POK: "On June 14, 2003, the then deputy prime minister, L.K.Advani told CNN that India needed to compromise with Pakistan and resile from extreme position to solve the Kashmir dispute.[26]

BJP when it was in power, made an incredible attempt to resolve the Kashmir problem and it would be uncharitable on our part if we do not acknowledge the endeavour of its leaders in this regard. But the ground reality is that Kashmir remains where it was six decades ago. Even beyond this it is moving backwards into oblivion. For this the failure of successive Indian Governments to evolve a well structured Kashmir policy is responsible. It is inevitable for us to accept that BJP led Government also did not do better than its predecessors to explore solid policy alternatives. Even the most articulate observer would find it difficult to elucidate New Delhi's Kashmir policy. Lacking a clear-cut direction, it has been a victim of confusion. The policy occasionally gets laced with bright patches which however do not take long to disappear owing to the Government's own lapses."[27]

**Janata Party**

The Janata party, which came to power in 1977, had a very definite position on Kashmir issue. There were widespread apprehensions that Janata party would bring in a fundamental shift in the nature and content of India's foreign policy specially the policy towards Kashmir. But contradictory to this, Janata party came with a clear and comprehensive policy position on the issue of Kashmir, which corresponds with the views of other national parties. At the outset, the Janata party accorded a top priority to Kashmir issue in its foreign policy agenda and it held an undisputed view that the whole of Jammu and Kashmir is an integral part of Indian union. The then foreign minister in the Janata Government, A.B. Vajpayee opined: "Jammu Kashmir is an integral part of India including the part occupied by Pakistan."[28]

The party favours the resolution of Kashmir dispute through mutual dialogue and did not favour a military solution. It opined that any solution to the problem must be found within the framework of the Shimla agreement. The Chinese interference in Indo-Pak equations was criticised by the Janata party as a factor that complicated the Kashmir problem. A.B. Vajpayee then foreign affairs minister expressed the view: "As regards Kashmir, there are two issues of the Chinese support of the self determination in Kashmir and the operation of the Karakoram highway across the Pak occupied Kashmir."[29]

Janata party has pointed out that restoration of normal bilateral relationship between India and Pakistan is to a large extent possible if Kashmir dispute is resolved. The founder of Janata party, Jayaprakash Narayan observed: "The question whether settlement of the Kashmir problem would establish friendship between India and Pakistan may be debated, but it cannot be denied that it will go a long way towards that goal."[30]

An analysis of the view of the Janata party reflects the aspect that its policies are somewhat similar to that of Congress. When it came to power, it did not entirely deviate from the course of action pursued by the previous Congress Governments. The party's conviction that the Kashmir dispute should be settled on the basis of Shimla agreement, exemplifies this notion. The only paradoxical opinion expressed by the party is on the question of Azad Kashmir or the Pak occupied Kashmir. On the one hand, the party claims that the whole of Jammu&Kashmir including the area occupied by Pakistan is an integral part of India. But on the other hand, it also expresses its view in favour of legitimising the boundary between India and Pakistan in Kashmir, by mutual friendship and co-operation. The party opined: "The boundary of Pak occupid Kashmir will gain legal validity only after the final settlement of the Indo-Pakistan dispute."[31]

**Janata Dal**

Janata Dal gives prominence to the socio-economic development and maintenance of political stability of Jammu and Kashmir. The party claims: "The Janata Dal led Government has paid special attention to the development of Jammu and Kashmir. In Jammu and Kashmir not only an elected Government was installed, but major initiatives were also taken to enhance the State's developmental activities."[32]

It held the view that rampant terrorist activities that have bred separatism in Kashmir leading to the issue becoming an intricate one. Hence a collective endeavour on the part of the entire nation is required to solve the acute domestic and external problems faced by Kashmir. The party argued: "Separatism is no answer to our problems, there is an urgent need for a national endeavour to solve the problem. A national effort will be made to resolve the complex problem like the Jammu and Kashmir."[33]

Janata Dal viewed that due to insurgency and terrorism, the

socio-economic development of Jammu and Kashmir has been paralysed. The party feels that due to the prevailing economic under-development and unemployment, the unrest among the Kashmiris intensified, compelling them to resort to militancy. Senior Janata Dal leader and former Prime Minister H.D. Deve Gowda said: "While militancy hindered tourism, loss of tourism led to great degree of unemployment and growing unemployment helped the growth of militancy, setting up a vicious circle."[34]

The party unequivocally claims that the whole of the territory of Jammu and Kashmir is an integral part of Indian Union and there will be no compromise with Pakistan over the issue. In view of this: "The then Prime Minister H.D.Deve Gowda ruled out any compromise with Pakistan over Jammu and Kashmir, saying that it is an integral part of India."[35]

An analysis of the policy position of Janata Dal towards Kashmir issue reflects some inconsistencies. At the outset, the stance of the party on holding a dialogue with Pakistan on the issue of Kashmir lacks definiteness and clarity of objective. It was stated in the Times of India: "Just days after emphasising at Jammu that Kashmir chapter was closed, in future discussions with Pakistan, the then Prime Minister H.D. Deve Gowda seemed to have changed his mind. In his felicitation message to Nawaz Sharif on his assumption of office as Pakistan's prime Minister, Mr. Gowda had said that, India was ready and willing to have wide ranging and comprehensive talks on all issues of mutual concerns."[36]

Further demonstrating his flexibility, "The then prime minister H.D.Deve Gowda said that he was prepared to discuss minor adjustments in relation to Kashmir within the scope of the Shimla agreement."[37] In spite of the claims of Janata Dal that Kashmir figures on the top of its agenda. The policies of the National Front Government headed by it, did not find any desired success. Balraj Puri opines: "The agenda of the National Front Government, as announced by Prime Minister, V. P. Singh in his first policy statement, accorded high priority to the Kashmir problem. But the situation in the sensitive border State sharply deteriorated under the new regime."[38]

**The Communist Parties**

The CPI criticised the Governments both at the centre and in Jammu and Kashmir for not evolving prudent policies to deal with the Kashmir problem, leading to its amplification. It is of the opinion that a national endeavour should be made to resolve Kashmir imbroglio. For this, a consorted effort should be made by political parties, social groups and individuals of the entire nation. The CPI states: "The present alarming situation in the valley of Kashmir is not a creation of a day. Actually the successive Governments, both at the centre and the State have, by their anti-democratic and anti-people policies, alienated large sections of people in the valley. The CPI appeals to all secular, democratic and patriotic forces in the country to mobilise public opinion in favour of resolving the vexed problem of Kashmir through a comprehensive policy."[39]

It is one among few political parties that has eloquently highlighted the issue of violation of human rights in Kashmir. The party argues: "there are many complaints of excesses and repression by security forces, which require to be looked in. Coupled with this the anti-human terrorist activities of the separatist forces had made the lives of the people of the State miserable."[40]

It is in favour of giving more autonomy to the State of Jammu and Kashmir. The party says that it is the only solution to bring the people out of alienation which they are being pushed into due to the long drawn politico-economic problems. It expresses: "Our party holds the view that for this, it is necessary to give maximum autonomy to Jammu and Kashmir, as well as regional autonomy to Jammu and Ladakh within this framework. For this, the centre should open a meaningful dialogue with Kashmiri leaders including the Huriyat and others."[41]

The Communist Party of India [Marxist] has been a staunch

advocate of the notion that U.S. machinations in connivance with Pakistan, has resulted in complicating the security situation in Kashmir. Indo-Pakistan tension has been utilised by the neo-conservatives in the U.S. administration for bolstering America's own imperial interests. The party observes: "The US administration is actively working behind the scene to promote the idea of an independent Kashmir."[42]

It further states that some pro-capitalist elements in the top political circles in India through their pro-American leanings have braced this US connivance with Pakistan. In this context the party blames the BJP Government that it demonstrated incapacity to resist US pressures, which was clearly highlighted during the Kargil conflict. The CPI [M] indicated thus: "The BJP led Government appealed to the US to intervene to resolve the conflict. This opened the way for American intervention and internationalising the Kashmir issue, because Pakistan had already fanned the intrusion in order to focus on the Kashmir issue."[43]

Ultimately the CPI [M] is an ardent critique of what it calls the incapability of Indian Governments to adhere to an independent foreign policy with relation to its neighbour Pakistan. The party believes that due to India's readiness to subjugate its national interest, to the imperial interests of the U.S under some sort of duress, the country's policy in Kashmir has been debilitated. Criticising the policies of the BJP led coalition Government towards Kashmir, the party pointed out : "Both on the vital question of Kashmir and India's role in the world, the BJP has compromised India's national interests by its willingness to become a junior partner of the Americans."[44]

An analysis of the attitude of Communist parties towards Kashmir issue indicates that the approach of both the parties is almost similar to each other. The position of both depends upon two significant aspects. Firstly, they are vociferous in criticising the policies of various Governments towards Kashmir. The parties share the common view that due to faulty policy formulations by the Government at the centre and the various Governments in Jammu&Kashmir, the problems of the State have mounted. Besides this, both the left parties are united in their criticism of the US role in the affairs of Indo-Pakistan relations. They have viewed that the Americans have pursued imperialist designs in South Asia by indulging itself in Kashmir issue. In addition to this both Communist parties have expressed serious concern about the human rights situation in Kashmir and hence firmly support the grant of more autonomy to Jammu and Kashmir.

An overview of the attitude of major national parties towards Kashmir issue denotes the consensus among all of them regarding the significance of the problem, for the conduct of India Pakistan relations. Their attitude on Kashmir issue can be designated into different categories.

**The Centrality of Kashmir Issue in India Pakistan Relations**

Indian political parties have expressed unanimous views regarding the significance of Kashmir issue in the realm of Indo-Pakistan relations. They accept the centrality of the issue among all other contentious bilateral issues enveloping their relations. Anyhow, they differ in their views regarding the means to be adopted for arriving at feasible solutions to solve the Kashmir issue and they have often indulged in criticising each other's policies towards Kashmir.

**Autonomy of Jammu and Kashmir**

Though there exists a consensus on Kashmir problem among political parties, there is no unanimity of opinion regarding the means to be adopted to solve the entanglement. For instance, almost all political parties agree that greater autonomy should be provided to Jammu&Kashmir. But the BJP is totally opposed to the grant of autonomy and in turn, it argues for the deletion of Article 370.

BJP's views have been inherited from its predecessor Jana

Sangh. This indicates the radical outlook of the right wing party. Anyway, after the party came to power, it considerably moderated its position on Article 370. This dilution corresponds with the attenuation of its Hindu nationalist ideological leanings, which was done keeping in mind the party's urge to run a coalition Government and remain in power. "At the party's April 1998 national executive meeting in New Delhi, Advani asked the party members to shelve the core idea of Hindutva, in the interest of producing a stable coalition Government."[45]

It appears that political parties view Kashmir problem from the prism of their ideology and not on the basis of ground realities. Hence, they involve themselves in criticism of other political parties. For example, the Communist parties view Kashmir problem from the perspective of their anti-imperialist ideology. Likewise, the BJP in its earlier days viewed the problem from the prism of its extreme Hindu nationalist ideology. So it called for the integration of Pak occupid Kashmir into Indian Union.

## Cross Border Terrorism and Human Rights

Political parties have a broad agreement that cross border terrorism has complicated Kashmir issue. They also agree that ending of cross-border terrorism is a prerequisite for the amicable solution of the Kashmir imbroglio. But they do not seem to arrive at a consensus regarding the nature and causes of terrorism and the policy alternatives needed to tackle the problem. Hence, India is not able to take concrete and effective steps to deal with the menace.

Similarly, the problem of human rights is a direct outcome of terrorism in Kashmir. But, it appears that though political parties express their understanding of the problem, they seem to have not defined it in a consistent and comprehensive manner, so as to focus on the policy prescriptions to counter the problem of human rights.

By and large, it may be opined that political parties have not made a united endeavour to engage themselves in a constructive role to discover concrete methods to resolve Kashmir conundrum. Hence there should be a joint endeavour on their part to decide on policies and measures for solving this long standing dispute. Maintenance of the continuity in the country's foreign policy transgressing partisan considerations will facilitate to a considerable extent the evolution of a stringent policy framework to deal with the various dimensions of this problem.

Such continuity has dawned in recent times, which has restored the aspirations of the people of the sub-continent, specially the Kashmiris, of a peaceful and prosperous future. This manifested in the launching of the Srinagar Muzzaffarabad bus service by the Congress led UPA Government; a policy initiated by the BJP led NDA Government. This symbolises the structural transformation in India's Kashmir policy, from being characterised by intense inter party squabbles to a constructive inter party cooperation.

## *References*

1. Indian National Congress, *resolution adopted at the 81st Plenary Session,* Bangalore, 17-18 March, 2001, p. 26.
2. Pandit Jawaharlal Nehru, *India's Foreign Policy*, Selected Speeches, September 1946 April 1961, Publication Division, Government of India, New Delhi, 1967, pp. 446-466.
3. Ibid., p. 466.
4. Indian National Congress *Manifesto*, Lok Sabha, Elections, 1999, p. 64.
5. Ibid., p.64.
6. Vayalar Ravi, *Rajya Sabha Debates,* 175(3), 29th November 1995, Rajya Sabha Secretariat, New Delhi, p. 318.
7. Indian National Congress *resolution adopted at the 81st Plenary Session,* Supra, 1, p. 26.

8. Indian National Congress *resolution adopted at the All India Congress Committee meeting* held at New Delhi, in May 2002, pp. 2-3.
9. Jaipal, Reddy, *Lok Sabha Debates,* Seventh Session, Thirteenth Lok Sabha, 18(13),Lok Sabha Secretariat, New Delhi, August 8, 2001, p. 265.
10. Manmohan Singh, *Rajya Sabha Debates,* 191(4), November 23, 2000, Rajya Sabha Secretariat, New Delhi, p. 200.
11. *Asian News Digest,* 5 (29), July 15-18, 2004, p. 3779.
12. Hari Jaisingh, *Kashmir A Tale of Shame,* UBS Publications, New Delhi, 1996 p. 9
13. Premnath Dogra, *Presidential address*, Third Annual Session of the BJS, Jodhpur, December 30, 1954, cited in Mohammed Ali Kishore, *Jana Sangh and India's Foreign Policy*, Associated Publishing House, New Delhi, 1969, p. 204.
14. Bharatiya Jana Sangh *Election Manifesto, general election 1958,*
15. Ibid.
16. Bharatiya Janata Party, *Election Manifesto,* general elections 1999, p. 35
17. Ibid., p. 35.
18. Madan Lal Khurana, *Lok Sabha Debates,* Seventh Session, Thirteenth Lok Sabha, 18(13), Lok Sabha Secretariat, New Delhi, August 8, 2001, pp. 265-266.
19. Bharatiya Janata Party, *Resolution adopted at the National Executive meeting* held at Vadodara on June 9, 1994.
20. L. K. Advani, *Presidential Address* BJP Plenary, Session at Bombay on November 10-12, 1995.
21. Jagmohan, *Rajya Sabha Debates* 75 (3), November 29, 1995, Rajya Sabha Secretariat, New Delhi, p. 341.
22. Bharatiya Janata Party, *Election Manifesto,* general election 1991, p. 8.
23. Bharatiya Janata Party, *Election Manifesto,* general elections 1999, p. 35.
24. Bangaru Laxman, *Presidential Address*, Bharatiya Janata Party National Council Session, 27-28 August, 2000, Nagpur, p. 13.

25. L. K. Advani, *Lok Sabha Debates,* Thirteenth Series, 3(13), December 15, 1999, Lok Sabha Secretariat, New Delhi, p.347.
26. *The Hindu,* 9th November, 2003.
27. B.K., Chum, *The National Herald,* 1st May 2001.
28. Atal Bihari Vajpayee, *The Statesman,* 23rd July 1978.
29. Ibid.
30. Jayaprakash Narayan, Our Great Opportunity in Kashmir, *The Radical Humanist,* 54(8), August 1978, p. 20.
31. K.P., Misra, [ed.], *Janata's Foreign Policy,* Vikas Publications, New Delhi, 1979, p. 206.
32. Janata Dal *Election Manifesto,* Lok Sabha Election 1998, p. 2.
33. V.P. Singh, *Social Justice for A Secular India,* Janata Dal Publications, New Delhi, 1990, pp. 1-2.
34. H.D. Deve Gowda, *Rajya Sabha Debates,* 185(17), 2nd August 1996, Rajya Sabha Secretariat, New Delhi, pp. 387-388.
35. H.D. Deve Gowda, *The Indian Express,* 14th February 1997.
36. H.D. Deve Gowda, *The Times of India,* 18th February 1997.
37. H.D. Deve Gowda, *The Times of India,* 24th February 1997.
38. Balraj Puri, The Challenge of Kashmir, *Economic and Political Weekly,* 35(4), January 27, 1990, p. 192.
39. Communist Party of India, *Resolution adopted at the 16th National Congress* held at New Delhi, 1995, pp. 139-140.
40. Communist Party of India, *Resolution adopted at the 18th National Congress* held at Thiruvanthapuram, March 26-31, 2002, p.64.
41. Ibid., p. 63
42. Communist Party of India [Marxist], *Resolution adopted at the 16th National Congress* held at Calcutta on 5-11 October 1998.
43. *13+4 Months of BJP Misrule Pokhran to Kargil,* CPI [M] Publications, New Delhi, p. 7.
44. Ibid., p.8.
45. *The Hindu,* 28 April 1998.

## Chapter 8

# Nuclearisation of India and Pakistan

Nuclear weapons constitute a major issue in the study of international relations. "Nuclear power has been described as 'at most deadly, a most dangerous process that man has ever conceived."[1] Nuclear weaponisation has become one of the major factors in international relations, having a potency to determine the nature and content of relations among different States of the world.

The presence of nuclear weapons poses serious ramifications for the bilateral and multi-lateral relations among States. Relations among States will be vitiated if any one of them possesses nuclear weapons and contributes to the heightening of tensions. According to Prakash Nanda there are significant similarities in the tensions between India-Pakistan, China-Taiwan and the two Koreas. He believes there are three common elements. "First is that, each case is a source of regional and global tensions. No wonder why so much of international media coverage is focused on them. Secondly, each one of these conflicts has a nuclear dimension. Thirdly, all these cases are conspicuous by the fact that the disputes relate to the unresolved dilemmas of their division."[2]

In view of this, emergence of India and Pakistan as declared nuclear weapon powers in recent times has brought in a structural change in the pattern of their bilateral relations. Nuclearisation of these States has acted as a catalyst in accentuating the already existing animosity between them. This has also magnetised an added global attention towards the South Asian region as, the obstinate belligerence between India and Pakistan has dragged their relations to a boiling point which engraves in it a perennial and potential threat of an open conflict involving nuclear weapons. "India and Pakistan are two nations that have experienced war with each other in 1947 over Kashmir, the Punjab area in 1965 and the Multan-Sindh-Kutch region in 1971. With an ever increase in weapons of mass destruction, South Asian region does not escape this trend. The increase of nuclear proliferation is evident in the nuclear programmes of both India and Pakistan."[3]

Hence today the nuclear factor has overshadowed all other aspects in determining the nature of Indo-Pakistan relations. The conflict prone nature of the politics of the sub-continent merits greater attention of the strategists to examine the present dynamics of India Pakistan relations, from the perspective of their newly assumed status in international politics.

**Evolution of India's Nuclear Programme**

The history of India's bid for the Acquisition of nuclear technology began to unfold immediately after independence of the country. "India's nuclear quest is tied to an accident of history, a confluence of two of the most striking personalities of our age- one belonging to the world of science and the other placed at the helm of political decision making. The two were none other than India's first Prime Minister Jawaharlal Nehru and India's great nuclear scientist and science organizer Homi J. Bhabha. Dedicated primarily to atomic power generation and other peaceful applications, India's nuclear technology acquisition kept the weapon option open."[4]

Jawaharlal Nehru's vision and Homi Bhabha's scientific skills ushered the era of nuclear technology in India. The process of India's nuclearisation went through a long period of gestation. "The full story of India's path to nuclear capability acquisition is bumpy but absolutely absorbing and spread over 50 years. Its special characteristic and the attached map will give glimpses intertwining atomic science and technology for peaceful application and the weapon option with overwhelming priority for peaceful uses."[5]

## Pokhran I Nuclear Test 1974

The first landmark in the chronicle of events in the history of India's nuclearisation is the peaceful nuclear explosion conducted by the Indira Gandhi Government in 1974 at Pokhran. The official claims regarding the Pokhran I nuclear test declared that nuclear explosion was carried out purely for peaceful purposes but the probability of the use of the weapon option was not ruled out. "The dominant motivations for this are regional in nature."[6] which compelled India to pursue a more robust nuclear policy.

"India's policy of nuclear abstinence underwent a definitive change after the first Chinese nuclear test in 1964. This shift in India's nuclear policy to nuclear ambiguity began with its own nuclear test, which was a watershed in India's nuclear decision-making."[7] On the other hand, "The primary justification for going nuclear was the perceived threat from a nuclear capable Pakistan."[8]

Whatever may be the external factors that played a vital role in shaping India's nuclear policy at the time of Pokhran-I, the significance of the domestic compulsions active at that time cannot be under rated. "India's ability to explode a nuclear device was demonstrated at Pokhran in May 1974. No single causative factor was underlying the Pokhran test. These were diverse and evolved over a period of approximately three years. Probably security threats, bureaucratic and scientific pressures and prestige considerations entered the decision-making process, but in different measures and in various points of time."[9]

"The decision to explode the device was probably dictated by technological and internal compulsions."[10] These included,

"The Atomic Energy Commission's determination to prove its metal and Indira Gandhi's sense that India would gain confidence in itself as a nation and in her as a leader. The final decision to conduct the test was the result of an *ad hoc* intuitive process that lacked a rigorous foreign policy analysis."[11]

**Pakistan's Nuclear Programme**

Here it is pertinent to know the roots of Pakistan's nuclear programme. "Pakistan has been rather slow and reluctant to start in the field of nuclear development. It was not until 1954 when the American exhibition on atoms for peace toured Pakistan that some interest was aroused in the potential of the new technology for national development. Consequently, a 12-member atomic energy committee was appointed by the Government of Pakistan to prepare a blueprint for the promotion of atomic energy in Pakistan. Based on the recommendations of the committee, an Atomic Energy Council was set up in March 1956, with the task of planning and development of atomic energy for peaceful purposes."[12]

Hence, with the establishment of Pakistan Atomic Energy Commission (PAEC), the nuclear programme of Pakistan was formally launched. "The efforts to achieve nuclear fuel cycle autonomy which is essential for developing a nuclear weapons option started in earnest only in the 1970s and gained impetus after the Indian nuclear test in 1974."[13]

At the dawn of the sixth decade of the 20$^{th}$ century, there emerged two schools of thought in Pakistan- one upholding the restriction of nuclear energy for only peaceful purposes and the other, preferring a more hawkish nuclear policy to discover its military uses. "Pakistan's actual nuclear history begins with General Ayub Khan's takeover of the Government in 1958."[14] This event is a benchmark in the history of Pakistan's nuclear programme. It was at this time that considerations of nuclear power for national development began to appear positive.

It was Pakistan's president General Ayub who was the first to express a political will to evolve a structured nuclear policy. "The Ayub regime was determined to promote the use of nuclear energy for peaceful purposes. However, it was sharply divided on its role for military employment. The Chairman of Pakistan Atomic Energy Commission (PAEC), Dr. I.H.U. Usmani, wanted to entail peaceful use ruling out any possibility of military use, whereas Z.A.Bhutto and his supporters were in favour of developing a nuclear capability that had potential for an eventual nuclear weapons option."[15] This was the era of intense political debate in Pakistan over the nuclear question and the divide within the ruling establishment regarding the usage of nuclear power generated immense heat and created frictions among the top leaders of Pakistani ruling class.

"Ayub seems to have finally accepted Usmani's view by rejecting Bhutto's suggestion."[16] Thus this was the initial years of Pakistan's nuclear programme and an analysis of these early significant events maps out for us the future shape and direction of Pakistan's nuclear policy. It also contributes to the understanding of the binding compulsions that led the policy makers of Pakistan to change the course of the country's nuclear policy from a peaceful one to the discovery of its military potential.

Here, it is significant to make a comparative analysis of nuclear programmes of India and Pakistan and while doing so, it seems that there exists a glaring incompatibility in the nuclear policies and pattern of national security strategies of the two. "According to a Pakistani analyst, the security models of India and Pakistan differ as their national aims and objectives are dissimilar. The nuclear postures of both India and Pakistan are different. Since such a stance is factored into the security perceptions of both the countries, it has consequently resulted in different nuclear doctrines and security paradigm."[17]

Pakistan's nuclear programme was moulded and influenced by one single factor that is its security threat perception from

India. "Pakistan's nuclear programme is reactive in nature, reactive to the developments in India. India's nuclear programme is not just a reaction to the Chinese and Pakistani nuclear programmes and military oriented right from the beginning, but it is also driven by the desire for prestige and international standing and India has a grand vision of its role in world affairs which visualizes that it cannot play effectively unless it acquires nuclear weapons."[18]

Hence, the Indian nuclear programme is broad based and takes into account global developments, as J. N. Dixit states: "India's nuclear policies have not developed in a vacuum. They are essentially a graduated and measured response to international non-proliferation trends which India perceived as a threat to its long term security interests."[19]

Contradistinguished to this, the Pakistani nuclear endeavour can be termed as Indo-centric. This manifests in the statement made by Z.A. Bhutto in 1965 when he boisterously argued in favour of weaponising Pakistan's nuclear capabilities. Bhutto's notions emerged out of his perturbations over the security threats to Pakistan due to its adverse relation with its militarily stronger neighbour India. He claimed: "If India developed an atomic bomb, we too will develop one, even if we have to eat grass or leaves or to remain hungry, because there is no conventional alternative to the atomic bomb."[20]. "This statement was fully endorsed by a cross-section of the Pakistani society, particularly the press."[21]

"In their book, *Islamic Bomb*, Steve Wiessman and Herbert Krosney assert that right from the mid-1950s, Zulfikar Ali Bhutto when he became a minister in Ayub Khan's cabinet was an advocate of Pakistan developing nuclear weapons. Pakistan's defeat in 1971 strengthened Bhutto's conviction. He took the decision that Pakistan should have nuclear capacity two years before India's 1974 test in Pokhran."[22]

Hence, Pakistan's nuclear policy can be viewed from the perspective of its troubled relations with India. The Pakistani ruling elite was driven into a megalomaniacal fantasy of achieving military parity with India by increasing its non-conventional weapons capacity, owing to its deep felt urge of achieving politico-strategic edge over its sub-continental adversary. By this the Pakistani ruling establishment felt that India would never be able to defeat Pakistan. In turn, Pakistan would attain leverage over India and hopefully at one point of time, it may inflict a military defeat upon India with the help of nuclear weapons.

**India Pakistan Relations in the Post Pokhran-I Period**

The Pokhran-I nuclear test by India drastically transformed the nature of bilateral relations between India and Pakistan. It heightened tensions, disturbed tranquility in the region and provoked Pakistan to take the root of military nuclear policy which finally has turned into a nuclear arms race between the two neighbours. It also attracted increased international observation towards the South Asian region.

On account of this, India and Pakistan got embroiled into an intense diplomatic altercation. Pakistan expressed a seemingly prejudiced view of the issue and made vociferous claims that its security is in jeopardy on account of India's nuclear test. On its part, India demonstrated remarkable discretness and tightly held on to its position that its nuclear explosions were conducted for peaceful purposes and it was not directed towards any country.

In her letter, the Indian Prime Minister Indira Gandhi stated that, "PNE is the normal result of the research and study of our scientists and we are firmly committed to the peaceful uses of nuclear energy. India has no military or political intentions in carrying out nuclear explosions."[23] On the other hand, the reaction of Pakistan's Prime Minister Z.A.Bhutto was replete with a nuclear threat perception from India. He remarked: "A more grave and serious event has not taken place in the history of Pakistan. The explosion has introduced a qualitative change in the situation between the two countries."[24]

Pokhran-I nuclear test ushered a covert nuclear competition and vitiated the bilateral relations of India and Pakistan. According to Zafar Iqbal Cheema: "Nuclear competition between India and Pakistan has proved intensely complex. The pattern of conflict in South Asia primarily between India and Pakistan has endured a cold war paradigm. The chances of de-nuclearisation of South Asia are slim because of the level of nuclear weapons capability."[25]

## India and Pakistan: The Road to Overt Nuclear Weaponisation

The intervening period between 1974 and 1998 marks an important phase in the history of nuclearisation of India and Pakistan. It is in these crucial years that both the countries catalysed their efforts to acquire weapons grade nuclear technology. This period is characterised by an aura of uncertainty, secrecy and mutual distrust over each other's nuclear capabilities. It is very significant to understand the 1998 declaration of nuclear weapons capabilities by both the countries in the light of the developments in these two decades.

In this period, a remarkable divergence can be witnessed in the nuclear policies of the two South Asian neighbours. India followed a policy of self-restraint or abstinence from further tests after 1974. But simultaneously, the Indian scientific establishment tacitly endured with its endeavours to achieve higher levels of nuclear technology without resorting to open tests. "In sharp contrast to India's reticence, Pakistan was garrulous in proclaiming its nuclear capabilities in the hope no doubt of deriving a measure of deterrence from its ambiguous nuclear posture."[26]

"The pattern of interactions between the two countries consisted of India's repeated denials of either possessing or wishing to possess nuclear weapons. Pakistan on the other

hand, interspersed jingoistic declarations that it possessed nuclear weapons with routing denials of any desire to weaponise its nuclear capabilities."[27] In this period, India lacked a coherent, clear, well coordinated and a circumspect nuclear policy. The period witnessed several perilous security situations that called for countervailing action that is, the situation compelled the policy makers to opt for open declaration of nuclear weapons capabilities. But the Indian policy makers felt rational enough in continuing with an undeclared nuclear posture. Hence, commenting on India's nuclear status before its open declaration, an assessment of the Russian intelligence concluded that, "India may be classified among the countries which unofficially possess nuclear weapons. There is an advanced programme of military applied research in the country. With stocks of irradiated fuel not under safeguard, the country could reprocess it for the purpose of extraction of plutonium for the creation of a powerful arsenal of nuclear weapons."[28]

But it seems that the policy pronouncements of successive Indian Governments before 1998 were broadly characterised by candid denials of having weaponised its nuclear technology. This policy stance of the Government has been comprehensively explained in a categorical statement of a former top Indian official that, "India does not possess nuclear weapons, consequently the military authorities have been directed to prepare plans to meet any foreign threat on the basis of our not having any nuclear weapons."[29]

The Government's self-imposed nuclear abstinence and the policy of deliberate nuclear ambiguity, ended only in 1998 after India crossed the nuclear rubicon and since then a serious endeavour has begun on the part of the Government to evolve a comprehensive and coherent nuclear doctrine.

Paradoxical to the Indian case, Pakistan's nuclear posture at this stage was entirely different. Its nuclear policy was characterised by a non-hesitant declaration of possession of nuclear weapons and a threat of use of nuclear power either preemptive or retaliatory, if there is a situation in which the country's national security was at stake. In this regard, the annual report of Indian Ministry of Defence viewed: "Pakistan continues to pursue a weapons- oriented nuclear programme. Pakistan Government, its scientists, officials and political leaders have openly accepted that Pakistan has acquired the capability of making nuclear bomb. Pakistan has reportedly acquired M 11 missiles from China which has a range of more than 300 kms and believed to carry nuclear warheads."[30]

In the decade from 1980 to 1990, Pakistan's capacity to produce and deploy nuclear weapons began to become more visible and explicit. Several hyper-nationalistic elements in the Pakistani politico-administrative set up, its military establishment, scientific community and the press indulged in articulations tinged with jingoism that their country possesses nuclear weapons and raised the specter of a likely Pakistani nuclear attack on India. "At least twice, speculations of an underlying threat of Pakistan resorting to the use of nuclear military power against India were aroused, following two significant crises in their bilateral relations. Firstly, during the Brass-tacks operations and secondly, when there was a massive mobilization of troops by both countries along the Indo-Pakistan border due to the augmentation of tension in the wake of the outbreak of militancy in Kashmir in 1990."[31]

Pakistan seems to have developed nuclear weapons capability prior to India. Since then it had a dubious distinction of having an undeclared nuclear weapons status. Contrary to this, India was passing through a phase marked by a syndrome of nuclear ambiguity. As a result, the nuclear picture of South Asia was enigmatic. This pendulous situation had brought in fears among various quarters in India, as the threat of an impending nuclear attack by Pakistan heightened.

## Pokhran-II and Chagai Nuclear Test 1998

"A critical question which assumes a silence in the light of developments [in 1998] relates to the implications of the overt nuclearisation of the sub-continent and more specifically what this entails in terms of regional stability."[32] It may be viewed that there occurred a basic shift in the security paradigm of the entire South Asian region after India and Pakistan conducted nuclear weapons tests in May 1998. It not only engendered a nuclear and missile arms race between India and Pakistan, but also brought a consequential impact upon the strategic calculus of the countries in the neighbourhood of India and Pakistan.

India's Pokhran-II nuclear test symbolised the culmination of a long process of scientific and technological endeavour to achieve a minimum credible nuclear deterrence. The event ended the state of strategic ambiguity which marked its nuclear security policy since the first nuclear test of 1974. "On 11 and 13th of May, India tested a total of five nuclear devices in the desert of Pokhran. The tests took the Indian public and the world by surprise."[33] "Simultaneous testing of a weaponised fission device, a low yield fission device and a thermonuclear device is an unprecedented event in the nuclear history."[34]

"The primary reason for declaring India's nuclear weapons capability was the perceived threats to it from the two hostile neighbours China and Pakistan."[35] Apart from this, "The detonation of nuclear devices at Pokhran is the result of its changing perception of threats to its national security. Sino-Pak nuclear nexus has provided valid reasons for India to break its nuclear restraint which it had observed since 1974."[36]

The most fundamental challenge faced by the Government after the nuclear tests was to evolve a coherent and comprehensive nuclear doctrine which would be acceptable in diverse sections of Indian society and would not rise skepticism in the international community. But a right perspective in this regard did not arise. Condemning the Government's attempt to initiate a debate over the draft nuclear doctrine, Muchkund Dubey observed: "The Government went to the extent of getting this draft made public even at the cost of antagonising some of our friendly countries and frightening others. In my view it was tactically very undesirable to have made a public announcement of the intentions based on plans and projects, some of which are still on the drawing boards and some of them are only in the form of conceptions."[37]

## Nuclear Testing by Pakistan

The immediate fallout of Indian nuclear tests was that a state of anxiety perforated the entire Pakistani society and the ruling establishment was exhorted from various quarters significantly, the army, the hawks in the scientific community and even the public, to match Indian action expeditiously. "Indian nuclear test questioned the credibility of Pakistan's deterrent capability. Huge domestic pressure in Pakistan left Nawaz Sharif with no option but to follow suit."[38]

On 28 and 30th of May 1998, Pakistan carried out nuclear tests at Chagai in Baluchistan. Prime Minister Nawaz Sharif announcing Pakistan's detonation of nuclear weapons device said that: "the decision was taken in the interest of national security and integrity and in this way now Pakistan had settled the score of strategic imbalance with India."[39]

## Post-May 1998 India-Pakistan Relations

Unlike the 1974 nuclear tests the implications of Pokhran-II for India Pakistan relations was deep felt and multi dimensional. It not only stimulated a similar response from Pakistan, but "The nuclear testing became a debacle issue in India and Pakistan. The Indian articulation focused on the threats from Pakistan and China while Pakistan targeted India."[40] "Since India has directly named China as its potential number one threat which led the former not to further delay testing of its nuclear bomb, dark shadows of the widening of India-China rift and India-Pakistan rift with Pakistan getting covert support from China have started appearing on the horizon."[41]

It was expected that overt nuclearisation would deter India and Pakistan from engaging in armed conflict due to the risk of accidental use of nuclear weapons. But paradoxically, the proxy war in Kashmir persists with several instances of open conflict, once in Kargil and secondly when the two countries were on the brink of a major armed conflict following the terrorist attack on India's parliament and the subsequent mobilisation of military on both sides of the border. In this context, it is generally considered: "Nuclear weapons do not contribute to stability in the region and further do not eliminate the possibility of a nuclear war in a nuclearised environment."[42]

The Kargil crisis of 1999, demonstrated this: "The Pakistan army mobilised its nuclear weapons against India without the knowledge of the then Prime Minister Nawaz Sharif."[43] This symbolises the growing complexities in their relations, stigmatised by a constant threat of inadvertent use of nuclear weapons. The prospects of arriving at an amicable solution to the protracted conflict appear remote. The situation becomes adverse due to the unclear articulation of their nuclear doctrines, the secrecy enveloping their nuclear posture and a policy of nuclear brinkmanship adopted by few leaders on both sides.

If any nuclear conflict occurs between India and Pakistan, the amount of human and material casualties will be unimaginable. Crucial fallout of the Indo-Pakistan nuclear weaponisation is that, "The nuclearisation has internationalised the Kashmir problem."[44] "Suddenly the nuclear tests in the sub-continent have brought the Kashmir issue to the core which is linked to any nuclear eventuality."[45]

Until India and Pakistan succeed in discovering solid mechanisms that could be instrumental in halting any probable nuclear conflict and if the paranoiac urge for nuclear might persists in the same frenetic pace, the region will be bogged down under a constant threat of a lethal war that would result in the emergence of neither victor nor vanquished, but only promises mutually assured destruction of both the countries. This uncertainty has also kept the entire sub-continent marginalized from the mainstream of socio-economic development.

A viable solution lies in building concrete trust between the two countries, but this is premised upon the amicable solution of the Kashmir dispute. As there exists an inevitable interface between the exasperated nature of the Kashmir conflict and the nuclear aspirations of India and Pakistan, however demure this inter-connection may be. Hence it may be underlined that the security, stability and prosperity of entire South Asia and its liberation from this nuclear consternation, largely depends upon the unraveling of the Kashmir entanglement.

## *References*


1. T. Shivaji Rao, *Environmental Impact,* Paper presented at a Symposium on the Nuclear Power, Costs and Relevance of an Energy Resources, Seminar 370, June 1990, p. 51.
2. Prakash Nanda, *Nuclearisation of Divided Nations, Pakistan-India-Koreas,* Manas Publication, New Delhi, 2001, p. 5.
3. Ajoy Ghosh, *Indo-Pak Conflict, Threat to South Asian Security,* Reference Press Publication, New Delhi, 2003, p. 1.
4. O. P. Sabherwal, India's Nuclear Strategy; Peaceful and Weapon Capability, *World Focus,* 19(9-12), Oct-Nov-Dec 1998, p. 20.
5. Ibid., p. 21.
6. Samina Ahmed, David Cortright and Amitabh Matto, Public Opinion and Nuclear Options for South Asia, *Asian Survey,* 38(8), August 1998, p. 744.
7. T.T. Poulose, India's Nuclear Option and National Security, in P. R. Chari, Parvaiz Iqbal Cheema, Iftekharuzzaman (ed.), *Nuclear Non-proliferation in India and Pakistan: South Asian Perspectives,* Manohar Publication, New Delhi, 1996, p. 42.
8. Samina Ahmed, David Cortright and Amitabh Matto, Supra, No. 7, p. 728.
9. P. R. Chari, *India's Nuclear Options : Future Directions,* in P.R.Chari,

Pervaiaz Iqbal Cheema, Iftekharuzzaman (ed.), Supra, No. 7, p. 62.

10. Onkar S. Marwah, "Comment", in John D. Mellor (ed.), *India Rising Middle Power,* Bolder, Colarado, Westview Press, 1979, pp. 216-217.
11. George Perkovich, *India's Nuclear Bomb – The Impact on Global Proliferation*, Oxford University Press, New Delhi, 1999, p. 146.
12. Naeem Ahmed Salik, *Pakistan's Nuclear Programme, Technological Dimensions,* in P. R. Chari, Pervaiz Iqbal Cheema, Iftekharuzzaman (ed.), Supra, No. 8, p. 87.
13. Ibid., p. 88.
14. Zafar Iqbal Cheema, *Pakistan's Nuclear Policies : Attitudes and Posture,* P.R. Chari, Pervaiz Iqbal Cheema, Iftekharuzzaman (ed.), Supra, No. 7, p. 105.
15. Zalmay Khalizad, Pakistan, in Joseph Goldblat (ed.), *Nuclear Proliferation,* The Why and Wherefore, Taylor and Francis, London, 1985, p. 133.
16. Zafar Iqbal Cheema, *Pakistan's Nuclear Policies: Attitudes and Posture,* Supra, No. 7, p. 105.
17. Kamal Matinuddin, Nuclearisation of South Asia: Implications and Prospects, *A Regional Studies*, 16(3), Summer 1998, p. 9.
18. Sandy Gordon, Capping South Asia's Nuclear Weapons Programme: A Window of Opportunity?, *Asian Survey,* 34 (7), July 1994, pp. 666-67.
19. J. N. Dixit, *India-Pakistan in War and Peace,* India Today Group, New Delhi, 2002, p. 330.
20. Z.A.Bhutto, *Awakening the People : Speeches of Zulfikar Ali Bhutto 1966-67,* Pakistan Publications, Rawalpindi, 1970, p. 21.
21. We must make the Bomb, *Dawn,* 30 September 1965.
22. Steve Wiessman and Herbert Krosney, *Islamic Bomb,* Time books New York, 1981.
23. *Amrit Bazar Patrika,* Calcutta, May 19, 1974.
24. *Patriot,* New Delhi, June 8, 1974.
25. Zafar Iqbal Cheema, Supra, No. 16, pp. 103-04.
26. *The Observer* (London), March 1, 1987.
27. Nawaz Sharif's, Bombshell, *India Today,* 15th September 1994, p. 47.

28. Russian Foreign Intelligence Service Report on Proliferation, unclassified State Department Message, 060611/01, dated 1st March 1993, pp. 1-3.
29. B.G.Deshmukh, The Inside Story, *India Today,* 28 February 1994, p. 62.
30. Government of India, Ministry of Defence, *Annual Report*, 1993-94, p. 3.
31. Based on *author's Interview* with former Defence Minister, George Fernandis, Allahabad, 15th August 2004.
32. M. Siddharth, Review Article, *Seminar*, 461(468), August 1998, pp. 87-88.
33. Kanti Bajpai, India's Nuclear Posture after Pokhran II, *International Studies,* 37(4), Oct-Dec 2000, p. 267.
34. Matin Zuberi, Pokhran II and Chagai, *World Focus,* 19(7-8) June-July 1998, p.8.
35. Based on *author's Interview,* Supra, No. 31.
36. Depankh, Chagai vs. Pokhran: A Road to Nuclear Vendetta, T*hird World Impact,* July 1998, pp. 13-14.
37. Muchkund Dubey's Interview on India's Quest for Credible Nuclear Deterrence and Stand on NMD, *Mainstream,* 39(21), May 12, 2001, pp. 5-6.
38. Ishtiaque Ahmed, Post-Pokhran Nuclear Politics, *The Radical Humanist,* 62(6), September 1998, p. 32.
39. Anthony Spaeth, *T*o Test or Not to Test, *Time,* June 1, 1998, p. 30.
40. Tehmina Mahmood, India and Pakistan's Nuclear Explosions: An Analysis, *Pakistan Horizon,* 52(1), January 1999, pp. 39-46.
41. Srikant Paranjpe, *India, Pakistan and Nuclear Tests*, *The Symbolism and Priorities*, *World Affairs,* 38(21), May 13, 2000, p. 13.
42. Charan D. Wadhva, Costs of Economic Sanctions: Aftermath of Pokhran II, *Economic and Political Weekly,* 33(26), June 27, 1998, p.1607.
43. M. Siddharth, Supra, No.33, p.88.
44. Syed Shahabuddin, Will Nuclear War Resolve the Kashmir Problem?, *Mainstream,* 40(27), June 22, 2002, p. 102.
45. Depankh, Supra, No. 36, p. 14.

## Chapter 9

# Attitude of Political Parties to the Nuclear Question

Nuclear testing by India and Pakistan has brought to the fore the vital question of the security and stability of the sub-continent. Magnifying the complexities of Indo-Pakistan conflict, the event has added a new dimension to the national debate on India's national security paradigm. Political parties which have been significant elements of the domestic political environment in India have been contributing consistently in this debate. Now this new phenomenon in the realm of India's security and external affairs has re-doubled the need for their active participation to provide a greater degree of meaning and substance to this crucial debate.

Several international variables influence the policy makers to adopt a strategy of nuclearisation. But the existence of numerous internal variables that contribute to this process cannot be undermined. Genuine national security concerns shape a nation's defence policy. A nation's national security paradigm is molded by diverse interests active in its domestic space. Prominent groups that represent broad opinion of the citizens, debate over the issue of national security and discuss whether nuclear weapons are conditional for effective safeguard of the country's security requirements.

This national debate conditions the perception of the policy makers and expedites the enactment of a rational defence policy. It also apprises them about the belief system prevalent in the nation regarding nuclear weapons. This coupled with the existing security environment, regionally and globally, forms the major inputs for the evolution of a nuclear defence policy.

In this context, political parties, as significant institutional variables, form one of the major domestic factors that have a prominent impact on the formulation of the defence policy. The perception of political parties regarding national security plays a vital role in moulding the defence policy of a country. Parties express their opinion as to whether nuclear weapons are needed for the protection of national security on the basis of their perception and evaluation of international situation.

In India, political parties have expressed a diverse opinion on the issue of nuclearisation of Indian defence mechanism and these views have significantly contributed to the shaping of India's nuclear policy. In the mid sixties, owing to the influence of the regional security environment, the issue of nuclear weaponisation became a notable subject of debate among political parties. "The technological sophistication manifested at Pokhran is a product of a long process of prioritisation of national security since the Sino-Indian war of 1962, and all mainstream political parties are culpable in ushering this political process."[1] In the light of this, it is pertinent to understand the approach of major national political parties towards the issue of nuclearisation of India Pakistan relations.

**Indian National Congress**

Since beginning, the party has expressed its aversion towards nuclear weapons. The party holds that its leaders have consistently laboured towards achieving a world free from nuclear weapons and the party's vision was to create a new world order free from nuclear weapons. The party believed: "It was Jawaharlal Nehru's vision that informed India's proposal to the United Nations General Assembly of a truly non-proliferation treaty. It was the same vision that inspired Indira Gandhi to launch the six nation initiative on nuclear disarmament. And it was the vision which found concrete and detailed expression in the action plan for a nuclear weapons-free and non-violent world which the Prime Minister Rajiv Gandhi submitted to the United Nations Special Session on Disarmament in 1988."[2]

In the context of cold war, the Congress party expressed its alarm over the ghastly process of arms build up by the super powers and felt that if it is not stopped by formidable means, then the entire mankind may be wiped out from the face of earth. A former president of INC, K. Kamraj Nadar said: "The great powers of the world have been arming themselves to the teeth with weapons of mass destruction. This mad race if not halted in time, must inevitably lead sooner or later to a conflagration, which unlike the previous world wars that left behind victors and vanquished, will exterminate all humanity."[3]

However, contrary to this position, it seems that the party had a very ambiguous stance on the issue of India's nuclear policy. The Indira Gandhi Government which carried out the 1974 nuclear tests, made arduous attempts to pacify domestic and international criticism by stating that Pokhran-I nuclear explosions were carried out purely for peaceful purposes. However, the secrecy surrounding India's nuclear motives, put the domestic public and international community in suspicion regarding India's actual nuclear posture.

It happened due to the policy of deliberate nuclear ambiguity maintained by the Congress both at the Governmental and the party level, leading to India's condemnation in various quarters that it was trying to indulge in nuclear weapon programme under the pretext of peaceful uses of nuclear technology. "The United States argued that no distinction could be made between a peaceful nuclear explosive and a weapon. India responded by rejecting US interpretation and asserted its right to pursue any peaceful application of nuclear energy including peaceful nuclear explosives."[4]

The party has reflected a relentless tilt towards peaceful uses of nuclear technology. It stated in its 1991 election manifesto: "The Congress is wedded to and will continue to, the use of atomic energy for peaceful purposes. Congress favours a nuclear weapons-free- world and will continue efforts for total and complete disarmament, particularly nuclear disarmament."[5]

But this position has not been manumitted from uncertainties. Antithetical to the party's firm commitment to the peaceful uses of nuclear energy, there have been moments when it has expressed inclinations for keeping the weapon option open. These manifests in the articulation of late Congress leader, Narasimha Rao, When he said : "today we have the choice of making or not making the bomb and I do not want to lose the option."[6]

Further it has attempted to justify its position of deliberate nuclear ambiguity on the pretext of the prevailing global nuclear apartheid practiced by the five established nuclear weapon powers. It had indicated that presence of these nuclear powers was a constant threat to non-nuclear powers like India. Hence the party maintained: "India cannot and will not surrender its nuclear option as long as security is threatened by the possessors of nuclear weapons and until such time as an agreement is reached on a just, equal, comprehensive and time-bound programme for the elimination of weapons of mass destruction."[7]

The party also has cited threats to India's national security, to substantiate its ambiguous nuclear posture. It remarked: "There are real and potential threats to our national security."[8] Although Congress party's views on nuclear weaponisation appears ostensible and it restrains itself from making an explicit demand for nuclear weaponisation, a definite tilt towards weaponisation as an inevitable option in times of grave crises infecting national security, can be cited. In this context, Pakistan factor has figured prominently in the party's perception on national security. The party holds: "In case Pakistan persists in the development or deployment of nuclear weapons, India will be constrained to review her policy to meet the threat."[9]

Pokhran-II nuclear tests seem to have resulted in a policy shift of the Congress, because the party hailed the tests and viewed that this technological accomplishment was materialised only due to the ground-work done by the Congress when it was in power. The party cited the technological feat India gained after Pokhran-I nuclear test of 1974, which laid the foundation for a formidable nuclear programme. The Congress thus eulogised: "The first Pokhran test of May 1974 was conducted during the prime-minister-ship of Indira Gandhi that was an assertion of the independence of our nuclear capability."[10]

Correspondingly, the Congress supported Pokhran II nuclear weapons test as a great attainment of Indian scientists and indicated that on this matter there was a national consensus. The Congress president Sonia Gandhi noted: "I would like to place on record in this formal meeting of the Congress working committee the pride we feel in the achievement of our nuclear scientists and engineers for putting India's nuclear capability in the front rank. We recall with equal pride that successive Congress Governments have ensured that India's nuclear capability remains up-to-date, so that our security is not compromised. The nuclear question is a national matter; not a partisan one. On this, every Indian stands united."[11]

The Congress regarded that the nuclear tests prognosticates drastic transformations in India's defence and foreign policy. The party felt that in such a situation, it was essential to re orient it in order to increase its adaptability to the changing circumstances. It observed: "The nuclear testing has brought a whole new dimension to our defence planning and strategy. The needs of the future will also be changing. With this in view, the Congress will appoint a High-Level Defence Reforms Committee to suggest a detailed operational plan for the re-organisation of the defence establishment in all its various aspects and for maximising the effectiveness of defence expenditure."[12]

Anyhow, the party has been vitriolic in its condemnation of the nature of post- Pokhran defence and foreign policy and dubbed it as abstruse, imperspicuous and lacking in objectivity. The party commented: "Our nuclear weaponisation programme remains a mystery. From all available evidence it seems more in the nature of enigmatic pronouncements than reality."[13]

After the Pokhran-II nuclear tests, the Government did not address several key issues. Firstly, on the question of the military applications of the nuclear capabilities, the Government's statement remained silent. The party remarked: "While Pokhran-II has established our weapon capacity and the question of weaponisation of our armed forces still remains which has to be done keeping in view the national security and economic considerations. Unfortunately, the Government has been vague, evasive and contradictory on the issue."[14]

The Congress severely condemned the BJP led coalition Government for not taking an objective and transparent stance on India's nuclear doctrine. The Government released the draft nuclear doctrine at the time of 1999 elections and at a moment when it had lost the confidence vote. The Congress viewed that it was merely a device to achieve a political gain. Lashing at the BJP led Government the present Foreign Minister Pranab Mukherjee had stated: "A Government which had lost people's mandate had no right to outline the policy, it is a poll gimmick. If the Government wanted national debate then it should have brought up the matter after the nuclear blast in 1998."[15]

It is significant to observe here that almost half way through its term in office, the Congress has not made any substantial headway in evolving a pragmatic and palpable nuclear doctrine. As a ruling party now it has to take into account its own criticisms that it had leveled as an opposition and act in an objective manner to engage itself in initiating a broad based national debate over India's nuclear doctrine.

The party had warned that the nuclear testing by India will considerably complicate the management of nation's foreign policy and relations. It further criticised the BJP led coalition Government that it carried out the nuclear tests without proper cognizance of the likely implications. Natwar Singh commented: "A great deal of excitement has been caused with the five nuclear tests and for the foreign policy of the BJP Government lays a great challenge. There is a difference between foreign policy and diplomacy. Foreign policy is what you do and diplomacy is how you do it. On both accounts, I do not think, this Government has taught through the consequences of its most recent action that is the dramatic explosions that have taken place."[16]

Congress opined that nuclear weaponisation has brought to the fore the question of maintenance of stable bilateral relations with Pakistan. Hence it is essential to put the issue of nuclear weapons at the top of the agenda of dialogue with Pakistan. The late Congress leader Madhav Rao Scindia had underlined: "Nuclear Risk Reduction measures must be put into place and they should be treated independently whether your talks on the other issues succeed or fail. There should be a different track for this. I would urge the Government to put in place machinery which can meet from time to time, exchange views, talk about safety measures and create a greater comprehension, at least, on this particular issue because the whole sub-continent is interested, all our neighbours are interested."[17]

The party believed that nuclearisation of India and Pakistan, has not resulted in a deterrent situation in South Asia. In turn it has been counterproductive and emboldened Pakistan's motivations that manifested in the Kargil crisis. "The plan was based on the fact that Pakistan had finally achieved parity with India after the nuclear tests the BJP conducted on May 11 and 13. This was done when Pakistan reciprocated with its nuclear tests in Chagai hills on May 28 and 30. The tests removed whatever restraints the Pakistani army had faced with respect to India's conventional military superiority."[18]

Hence the party advocated that "Concrete steps have to be taken to ensure that the nuclear weapons available with India and Pakistan are never used. At the same time, we must never allow a nuclear arms race to develop in the region."[19] The party also emphasised: "Management of India's relations with other nuclear weapons powers is an important task, given India's nuclear weapons and missiles capacities. Special attention should be paid to enhance India's credibility as a responsible nuclear weapons power and forging equations with other such powers to stabilise the international security environment."[20]

It is pertinent to note here that the Congress Government has come to power, but still there appear no symptoms of the Government devicing a concrete plan to deal with the problems that have arisen after the nuclearisation of India and Pakistan. This renders the criticisms and policy suggestions that it had made in this regard as an opposition to be an empty rhetoric. The aim of the present Indian regime must be to reiterate in its dialogue with Pakistan, the resolve made by both the Governments in the Lahore declaration to take heedful steps to reduce nuclear accidents and the risks of unauthorised use of nuclear weapons and their commitment for no first use;. The Government in a summit meeting with Pakistan should persuade its leaders to arrive at a comprehensive agreement that inscribes all these aspects.

An overview of Congress's views on the nuclear issue indicates that its position has been pendulous, oscillating between two extremes; peaceful uses of the nuclear energy and the exercise of the weapon option. The party has been indecisive in expressing its views on the Pokhran nuclear tests. On the one hand it maintained: "Without planning to the country then or subsequently what its compulsions were for abandoning the tried and tested posture towards the acquisition of nuclear weapons, Pokhran-II was presented to the nation and the world as a fait accompli which took us over the nuclear weapons threshold. Our response with Pokhran II and the ambiguous doctrine of 'Minimum credible deterrence' seem to have impressed neither the five traditional members of the nuclear club nor the Non-Aligned movement, nor indeed our neighbour."[21]

Paradoxically, the party has expressed its mute acceptance to the weaponised nuclear posture that resulted after Pokhran-II by declaring: "Congress is committed for the maintenance of a minimum credible nuclear program."[22]

Further, Congress's position gets more obfuscating when at one instance it hailed Pokhran-II as a brilliant technological accomplishment of the Indian scientists. It also claimed that the ground work which had been done by the previous Congress Governments, since the Pokhran I in 1974, is the fundamental reason for the present success. On another instance, the party takes a U turn and condemns the tests as a fait accompli.

It may be deduced here that the party's acclamation to Pokhran II was merely a knee- jerk reaction to the prevalent domestic mood that was tinged with hyper-nationalistic impressions. Congress and almost all other parties attempted to follow a mass hysteria that was prevalent at that time. But when international responses turned hostile and Pakistan also reacted with its nuclear tests, the support of the party totally diluted.

In addition to this, the party's stance that after 1974 nuclear tests, their Governments maintained strict restraint with regard to conducting nuclear tests is not factual. "Twice under the Congress regime it was decided to carry out nuclear tests."[23] First around 1982-83 Indira Gandhi decided to carry out test, but she herself withdrew at the last minute. Secondly, P. V. Narasimha Rao in 1995, held back the test because the CIA was able to detect the preparations of the tests.

Congress Government in nearly four decades of its rule did not clearly delineate the contours of India's nuclear policy. It was sandwiched between two half baked notions of global nuclear disarmament and credible nuclear deterrence for India's national security. Now the time is ripe to put things in order and evolve a concrete nuclear doctrine for the country. Since the party is presently in office, it has an opportunity to reshape India's defence and foreign policy to suit its status of a declared nuclear weapons power. The Indo-U.S. civilian nuclear deal initiated by the Congress led UPA Government appears to be the first heedful step towards assertion of India's position as a nuclear power and end the policy of deliberate nuclear ambiguity, followed with much sincerity for about half a century.

**Bharatiya Janata Party**

BJP's views on the nuclear issue, finds its roots in the ideas of its predecessor the Jana Sangh. The latter had perceived, nuclear environment in India's neighbourhood, the entry of cold war into the bounds of South Asia after Pakistan's military alliance with the US, resulting in the deterioration of the security situation of the region; as serious compulsions for India to attain a credible nuclear weapons capability.

In a meeting of eminent scientists, academics and politicians on India's nuclear policy, organised by the Indian parliamentary and scientific committee in May 1970 at New Delhi, several participants, urged the Government to revise its policy and produce nuclear weapons. "They argued that India's prestige and national security depended on nuclear weapons. Among them the Jana Sangh was the most vocal pro-bomb party."[24] Its leaders vociferously argued in favour of India attaining a nuclear weapons capability. Subsequently, "India exploded its first nuclear device in May 1974. Jana Sangh leader A.B. Vajpayee was among the first to extol this decision."[25] Here lie the springs of BJP's views on the nuclear issue. It may be noted that the party's candid tilt towards nuclear weaponisation is a legacy derived from the Jana Sangh.

Since inception, BJP has been an ardent proponent of India exercising its nuclear option through weaponisation.

Concurrently, it has also expressed its strong conviction that achievement of world peace is premised upon total disarmament both nuclear and conventional. Angst over the nuclear arms race between the two super powers in the cold war era, the party expressed: "It is incumbent on the super powers to move purposefully towards nuclear disarmament. What is at stake is not just their respective domains, it is the entire humanity."[26]

Asserting the sovereign rights of all free nations to decide upon the priorities to be adopted for protecting their national security, the party condemns the discriminatory global nuclear regimes. Articulating his views, L.K. Advani said: "We are unable to accept the thesis that the national security of some can dictate even a continuation of nuclear tests that too despite the NPT, India' security requirements are such that they can always be relegated to a position of irrelevance. We regard the NPT and its recent extension and ratification as an iniquitous arrangement India must reserve to itself all rights to take decisions as are in the interest of the nation."[27]

Further Advani believed that acceptance of this nuclear apartheid will totally bridle India's options to preserve its national security. Specially in the wake of a threshold nuclear weapons State Pakistan striving for a nuclear deterrence in order to blunt India's conventional military superiority and a declared nuclear weapons power China, attempting to tilt the regional balance of power in its favour through a policy of brinkmanship by virtue of its having a proven nuclear weapons capability.

Hence for India, it was imperative to devise countervailing strategies like developing a credible nuclear weapons deterrence in order to face the challenge. He also remarked that the end of cold war has not resulted in the elimination of nuclear threats to the world. He viewed: "Globally there has been some welcome movement forward, regionally; however, the problem of proliferation has got aggravated. With Pakistan self-declaredly a nuclear weapons State, given the reality of a nuclear People's Republic of China and the aspirations of some nations in the

Gulf, and the turmoil and uncertainty within the Commonwealth of Independent States, India has to address itself to this question principally as one of national security concerns. We cannot acquiesce in any effort to "contain India." Our policy in this regard is dictated by continuity and more so, by a need for deterrence against aggression."[28]

In this context the BJP as an opposition disapproved the then Indian Governments foreign policy and maintained: "For over four decades India's foreign and defence policies have lacked clarity and are devoid of objective understanding of the conditions of the world. India did not wake up when China after humiliating her in 1962 went on to become a nuclear power in 1964. Even now in the light of Pakistan emerging as a nuclear weapons State, the BJP has demanded that India must exercise its nuclear option so as to meet any threats to its security."[29]

These ideas emanated from BJP's solemn conviction that Pakistan had acquired nuclear weapons capacity prior to that of India and this advantage emboldened the latter to pose more serious challenges for India's national security. The party had observed: "Pakistan is now a nuclear weapon State and this fact changes the military equation in Hindustan Peninsula. The Government of India must take any and all measures including the exercise of nuclear option to meet Pakistan's challenge to India's territorial integrity."[30]

Hence, the BJP consistently counseled in favour of India exercising its nuclear option and weaponise its nuclear capacity, on the grounds of perceived threats from adversaries in the neighbourhood. L.K.Advani argued: "So far as the BJP is concerned, it would like to reiterate its view that against the background of China and Pakistan having become nuclear powers, national security warrants that India too must develop a nuclear deterrent of its own."[31]

This has also been the party's popular agenda. 1996 election manifesto of the party declared: "The BJP will set up a national security council; re-evaluate the country's nuclear policy and exercise the option to induct nuclear weapons."[32] It is in this perspective that Pokhran II must be visualised and on this pretext, the BJP led coalition Government justified the tests.

The Bharatiya Janata Party celebrated the tests as a remarkable achievement of the scientific establishment and it viewed that it was an audacious expression of the country's national interest. It claimed: "The BJP national executive hails the successful nuclear tests conducted by the BJP led Government as a bold and decisive decision in the right direction. Pokhran-II has not only demonstrated that India's indigenous scientific talent is second to none but also provided the nation with a deterrence capability. For long India has had a genuine security concern. These concerns, neglected for more than two decades, have been addressed."[33]

When economic sanctions were levied upon India, the BJP expressed its conviction that India had the courage and capacity to counter the challenge. The party had stated: "As expected economic measures have been taken against India for daring to challenge the discriminatory arrangements. But India's spirit cannot be broken by sanctions or by initiating punitive steps. India has the strength and capacity to withstand and survive economic sanctions."[34] In this context, C. Rajamohan observed: "The post-Pokhran U.S. sanctions lasted barely three and half years and have hardly affected the Indian economy."[35]

Hence Pokhran-II was the first clear expression of India's nuclear policy depicting a bias for military applications of nuclear power. It got liberated from the syndrome of deliberate nuclear ambiguity that marked India's nuclear policy for nearly five decades. The antagonists of Pokhran II argued that Pakistan reacted with its nuclear tests plainly as a response to Indian tests. Cracking down these arguments in parliament A. B. Vajpayee the then Prime Minister responded: "Some hon'ble members have said that, Pakistan conducted the tests in response to India's tests. Is a nuclear test possible within a short period of 16 days?"[36]

By this Vajpayee intended to illustrate that Pakistan had adopted a vicious posture against India and had a deep felt urge to achieve military parity with it. For this Pakistan had chosen the path of nuclear weaponisation, much before the Indian tests of 1998. With these arguments, the former Indian Prime Minister also had attempted to rationalise Indian tests as timely and any dereliction in this regard could have costed heavily for India's national security interests.

The critics also alleged the BJP led coalition Government of destroying the democratic process of national consensus, by taking a unilateral decision to carry out nuclear tests. Amrita Abraham reflects the mood of the critiques thus: "The strategic doctrine that drove the nuclear tests in Pokhran was made in the inner Bharatiya Janata party circles long before it came to power. With the possible exception of the defence minister, none of the other parties who formed the Government had contributed to the decision, nor the opposition, nor the informed public opinion. Rational policy making, the consultative process, consensus-building and collective responsibility are exploded by the five tests. The first casualty of an assertive nuclear policy is democracy. A sound national consensus on India's nuclear policy is over turned by a shaky and inexperienced coalition."[37]

In defence of this A.B. Vajpayee maintained: "The whole country had welcomed Indiraji's decision of granting permission for conducting tests. Her decision was not a collective decision. She did not consult the opposition for conducting the tests. But her decision was right and was in the interest of the country's security."[38] Vajpayee vindicated the Governments decision by contending that crucial policy decisions involving acute questions of national security if enacted with some degree of confidentiality, does not rupture the democratic process, as long as it serves our national interest.

Thus the emergence of Bharatiya Janata Party in the mainstream of Indian polity indicated a radical transformation in the debate over the country's nuclear policy. The party was the forerunner among those who favoured a nuclear policy directed towards weaponisation right from the days of its predecessor Jana Sangh. Its advocacy that India must use its nuclear option is corroborated on the perceived security threats by the presence of nuclear neighbours.

With such a vociferous articulation regarding the perceived security threats from China and Pakistan and declaring them as India's primary enemies and championing the need for India adopting a nuclear weapons posture. The party may benightedly contribute to the accretion of insular tendencies among the citizens through such hyper nationalistic campaigns. Besides, the adherence of BJP to the idea of universal nuclear disarmament as propagated by its senior leaders on the one hand and interspersing jingoistic arguments in favour of India developing nuclear weapons on the other is paradoxical. This renders the party's views to be devoid of objectivity.

There was a nationwide debate over whether or not the BJP led-coalition Government should have taken the unprecedented step of breaking the nuclear barricade and terminating the long standing ambiguity over India's nuclear policy. Unlike the 1974 tests, where in the Congress Government claimed that they were done for peaceful purposes, Pokhran II was proffered to the nation as a valorous step in the direction of preservation of our national security. It appears that the BJP led coalition Government exaggerated upon its stance. No doubt, there is a long drawn security threat to India from its hostile neighbour Pakistan and it was amplified when the latter acquired a covert nuclear capability but the prospects of Pakistan using nuclear weapons against India seemed to be bleak, simply because of the devastating effects of such an adventure, not only upon whom it is used but on the user too.

In addition to this, there is a strong international opinion against nuclear weapons after the catastrophe of Hiroshima and Nagasaki. Apropos China, it can be viewed that acquisition of nuclear weapons by it has neither adversely effected Sino-Indian security equations, nor did Indian nuclear weaponisation resulted in their relations assuming a cold war paradigm. "Notwithstanding the adversarial relationship that has existed between India and China, there has not been a single instance of nuclear threat or blackmail by China against India despite a long-standing border dispute. There has been no ideological confrontation between the two nations like the one that existed between the US and Soviet Union during the cold war years. India has been living with the Chinese bomb since 1964."[39]

Overall "In the more than five years since India and Pakistan in that order declared themselves nuclear weapons States, there has been no evidence that the acquisition of nuclear arms has strengthened security in South Asia."[40] Indo-Pak confrontations in Kargil exemplify the fact that a situation of weaponised deterrence has not been created in the region. The unrelenting Pakistani proxy war resulting in a persistent conflictual posture of the two nascent nuclear States that manifested in various instances such as their military mobilisation on both sides of the border in 2002, prognosticating a devastating war, provides credence to our arguments.

Hence the logic of Bharatiya Janata party's security threat perceptions that stimulated its Government's decision to cross the nuclear rubicon is questionable. I.K.Gujral, former Prime Minister believed: "There was no security compulsion for doing the tests, I am saying this because I was the Prime Minister, I am saying this because I knew everything, and I am saying this because in this country only the Prime Minister is the privy to certain secrets which nobody else is. And I say this with a sense of responsibility that there was no security compulsion for performing the test."[41]

Finally, after the BJP led coalition Government conducted the nuclear tests; it did not attempt to address several basic questions that emerged as a result of the tests. Prominent among them were the question of formulation of India's nuclear doctrine, the problem of nuclear weaponisation of the armed forces and setting up of the nuclear command and control. The BJP led coalition Government did not answer these questions satisfactorily. Now as an opposition, the onus falls on the party to exhort the present Government to appropriately deal with these crucial questions and formulate a concrete policy framework that suitably addresses these problems.

**Janata Party**

The short period of the Janata Party in the mainstream of Indian politics and its brief stint as the ruling party at the centre, constrained the party from widely articulating its views on nuclear policy. It has not maintained its party documents systematically, primarily due to its disintegration. Whatever was available have been used to make some observations on its attitude on the nuclear question.

A first sight of the Janata Party's stance on the nuclear policy, demonstrates its profound aversion towards nuclear technology, be it even for peaceful purposes. Immediately after it assumed office at the centre in 1977, the then Prime Minister Morarji Desai stated in his first press conference on March 24, 1977: "If it was not necessary to have nuclear explosion for peaceful purposes, then it should be never done."[42]

However, its policy position on nuclear issue demonstrated lack of objectivity and consistency. Desai stated on May 15 in another press conference: "If a peaceful nuclear explosion was necessary, India will do it. But we will not do in hide and seek manner. We will tell the people that we are doing and let them come and witness and the use will also be open equally to others."[43] "There was also an effort to demonstrate India's genuine intention about the future explosions, if any, being for purely peaceful purposes."[44]

There was a further shift in this position when the then prime minister told the Lok Sabha on 13 July: "No further explosions are necessary to be carried out now by India for purposes of harnessing nuclear energy for peaceful purposes."[45] On 22 December, Desai reaffirmed in the Rajya Sabha: "India was committed not to explode any nuclear device for peaceful purposes or make any nuclear weapons."[46] "The shift in India's stand was there for any one to see."[47]

However, the Janata Party's position on the NPT seemed to be firm and consistent. In this regard, it viewed: "As far as the NPT is concerned, we congratulate the Government on the bold stand taken that we will not sign the NPT because it is discriminatory."[48]

Thus it may be viewed that the nuclear policy of Janata Government did not bear much impact on India's nuclear programme in terms of content and direction. It lacked a clear stance that was needed at that moment when India had conducted peaceful nuclear explosion and there was a widespread national and international debate pertaining to India's nuclear policy. The Janata Government also did not clearly articulate the likely impact of the nuclear factor on India's relations with Pakistan in the light of Pokhrán I and did not propose any policy alternatives to deal with such a situation, if it were ever to emerge. This illustrates the lack of vision in the Janata party regarding the nuclear question.

Hence, it may be viewed that the study of Janata Party's nuclear policy does not assume much significance. According to P.R. Chari the Janata Party's nuclear policy was as follows: "The nuclear policy of the Janata Party, which came to power in 1977, as fore stands : "India would utilise atomic energy for peaceful purposes only, and would not manufacture nuclear weapons under any circumstances; India would not sign the Non-Proliferation Treaty unless the nuclear weapons powers renounce these weapons; inspection of autonomously controlled or domestically established nuclear facilities would not be permitted; and peaceful nuclear explosions would not be conducted and their utility is questioned. The first three stance of the Janata Government's nuclear policy correspond to previous Government's position, but a sharp difference is evident in its attitude towards peaceful nuclear explosions. This aspect of the Janata

Party's policy has been criticised as a "surrender of national autonomy by opposition groups."[49]

**Janata Dal**

The problem of analysing Janata Dal's nuclear policy is the same as that of the Janata party. Due to its short existence in the national scene and its subsequent degeneration owing to fragmentations it was not able to play any vital role in the formulation of India's nuclear policy. The party was not able to comprehensively articulate its views regarding the questions relating to nuclear policy. Hence, Janata Dal's nuclear policy was not clear. However, with the help of the statements of some JD leaders and a few party documents, an attempt has been made to understand Janata Dal's approach to the issue.

Janata Dal opposes the CTBT and NPT and dubbed them as discriminatory arrangements. Defining its position the party stated : "The Janata Dal will not accept any discriminatory approach on matters pertaining to international armament and disarmament questions. Therefore, the Janata Dal will continue to oppose the NPT and its adjunct the CTBT as they are discriminatory and aimed at the preservation of the hegemony of a few countries. At the same time, we will continue to work for a comprehensive and complete nuclear disarmament through the elimination of all weapons in the world."[50]

It may be noted that the position of Janata Dal on nuclear policy is plagued by internal contradictions. For instance, the attitude of the party towards CTBT is not consistent. The party stated in its manifesto that it is totally opposed to the arrangement since it is discriminatory. But the opinion and comments of various leaders of the party do not reflect unanimity. For example, if the former Janata Dal president Lalu Prasad Yadav, opposed signing CTBT and said: "India should not sign the Comprehensive Test Ban Treaty [CTBT] under any pressure."[51] I.K. Gujral the former prime minister "called upon the Government to sign the CTBT."[52]

Further, the views of various leaders of the JD on Pokhran-II nuclear tests are also marked by internal contradictions. Senior Janata Dal leader and former Prime Minister Deve Gowda supported the tests. "He congratulated the scientists for successfully carrying out the nuclear tests at Pokhran."[53] Paradoxically I.K. Gujral reprobated the tests as political gimmick guided by partisan considerations. He emphasised: "There may be another consideration, there may be political considerations, there may be partisan consideration, but security consideration was definitely not there."[54]

In the ultimate analysis, it may be viewed that due to paucity of adequate literature like the party documents regarding its attitude towards India's nuclear policy, we have been constrained from making a comprehensive analysis of Janata Dal's position on nuclear issue. An assessment of the statements made by various leaders indicates to the lack of consensus in the party on the nuclear issue.

The party also has not given proper emphasis on the implications of growing Pakistani assertion in the 1980s and 1990s of possessing nuclear weapons upon the security of the sub-continent and skepticisms of its possible use against India. During this period, the party was at the helm of affairs in national politics and this was the time when Pakistan's candid nuclear motivations became apparent. The party's over indulgence in domestic politics might have constrained it from a heedful expression of its views on the nuclear debate prevalent at that time.

**Communist Party of India**

The essence of CPI's views on nuclear policy is its anti-American attitude. The policy pronouncements of the party focus more on condemnation of American imperialism and its machinations which the party believes is solely responsible for pushing the entire mankind to the brink of a threat of nuclear war. While doing this, the party exhibits solidarity with the communist fraternity, like China and Russia. The party maintained: "Bush's nuclear posture review calls production and use of a new generation of nuclear weapons directed against China, Russia and five other nations. To wage this never-ending war, Bush administration has asked for a 48 billion dollar increase in the military budget including funds for the development of his so-called missile defence programme of nuclear weapons in space. The 18th Congress of the CPI condemns the U.S. imperialists' nuclear war policy."[55]

Opposing the global nuclear regimes, the CTBT and NPT, the party stated that they are antithetical to nuclear disarmament. Dubbing them as an attempt on the part of US to perpetuate its hegemony, the party argued: "The recent New York Conference on NPT has unanimously decided on indefinite extension of the NPT. It means that the signatories to the NPT have consciously opted out of any nuclear disarmament policy and the concept of the CTBT has been buried fathoms deep."[56]

The CPI criticised the BJP led coalition Government's decision to carry out nuclear tests at Pokhran as a politically motivated decision which reflected the party's myopic vision of India's national security. The party holds the view that in doing this, the BJP Government not only has ignored the actual problems of the country, but the tests also instigated Pakistan to reciprocate, spurring an arms race in the region. This has adversely effected the bilateral relations of India and Pakistan. According to the party: "obsessed from its very birth by the thought that the possession of nuclear weapons would symbolise a strong and powerful India, the BJP Government hastened to carry out the Pokhran tests soon after it came to power forgetting the fact that it was to eliminate poverty and economic distress and strengthen economic might and social stability. The theory of credible nuclear deterrence only gave false sense of security and was even responsible for neglect in other aspects of strengthening security, both military and economic."[57]

Finally the party has viewed that "India should pursue a policy of universal nuclear disarmament and nuclear free zone in South Asia."[58]

It may be opined that CPI has viewed the nuclear question from the prism of its anti-imperialist ideology. The party holds that Indo-Pakistan relations have been vitiated by the machinations of the imperialist forces sphere headed by the U.S. leading to the nuclearisation of the region. But paradoxical to its calls for universal nuclear disarmament, the party supports the creation of a nuclear free zone in South Asia. It is contradictory to the official Indian position of global approach to the question of nuclear disarmament. From a long time, Indian Governments, be it of any party, have favoured a universal nuclear disarmament and opposed a regional, that too a South Asian perspective of nuclear disarmament. This is because presence of a nuclearised China is a potent factor determining India's national security equations, specially after the latter's confrontationist approach that was demonstrated in 1962.

**Communist Party of India [Marxist]**

Like the CPI the CPI [M] has also viewed the nuclear question from the perspective of its anti-imperialist ideology. Condemning the global nuclear regimes such as the CTBT and NPT as emblems of U.S. imperialism, which it intends to impose upon India, to perpetuate its neo-imperialist designs. The party holds: "The USA has mounted sustained pressure to force India to sign the Nuclear Non-proliferation Treaty or a regional treaty on proliferation."[59]

The party criticised the then BJP Government as pro-American and commented: "The Vajpayee Government is not moved by any anti-imperialist principles. It is willing to sign the CTBT to appease the US."[60]

Further the party condemned the BJP Government that it compromised the fundamental principle of India's foreign policy of non-alignment, in order to brace its connections with the imperialist U.S. The party noted: "Within a short period, the BJP-led Government has reversed the course of India's foreign policy, whose foundations were based on non-Alignment and independence in decision making. After the Pokhran tests, faced with international isolation, the Vajpayee Government began succumbing to US pressures in its anxiety to get acceptance as a nuclear weapon power."[61]

The party believes that BJP's decision to conduct nuclear tests were driven by its Hindutva ideology. Senior CPI [M] leader Harkishan Sing Surjeet noted: "RSS and BJP's predecessor, the Jana Sangh, have been demanding that India should make the nuclear bomb. This fits in with the RSS-Hindutva ideology and scheme of things."[62]

It also criticised the BJP Government that it used nuclear brinkmanship as a lever in Indo-Pakistan equations. The party viewed: "The politbureau of the CPI [M] strongly criticises the statement made by the then home minister L.K. Advani, linking the finding of a lasting solution to the Kashmir problem to India becoming a nuclear weapons State. To indulge in nuclear saber-rattling to deal with Indo-Pakistan relations is totally unwarranted, which can lead to dangerous consequences."[63]

The CPI [M] condemned the BJP Government that its decision to weaponise India's nuclear capability resulted in the deterioration of the security situation in the region. Due to this Indo-Pak tensions have been aggravated, as the nuclear tests have engendered a nuclear arms race between them. The party remarked: "The decision of the BJP-led Government to go in for nuclear weaponisation after the tests in Pokhran in May, 1998, marked a dangerous new phase in India's external and nuclear policies. It has created the situation for a nuclear arms race in the sub-continent with Pakistan responding to India's nuclear tests."[64]

The party also condemned that Pokhran II has radically transformed India's established nuclear policy that too with out a national consensus. It argued: "The Vajpayee Government has surreptitiously and illegitimately reversed long-standing nuclear policy of the country."[65] The party also holds that the nuclear tests internationalised India's bilateral issues and India has become more vulnerable to imperialist pressures. Defining its position, the party indicated: "The Vajpayee Government's policy of nuclear weaponisation after the Pokhran tests, in May 1998 has made India more vulnerable to imperialist pressures. The US is playing the role of arbiter in the Indo-Pakistan nuclear equations."[66]

The party affirms that Pokhran-II created a weaponised deterrence in South Asia at the cost of India's long standing conventional military superiority and provided a strategic advantage to Pakistan. The party observed: "All that the BJP achieved was to have brought Pakistan on an equal footing with India in the international arena. Pakistan was inferior to India on various counts, particularly in the sphere of conventional weapons, but once Pakistan responded to Pokhran II with nuclear tests in Chagai, it achieved nuclear parity erasing India's superiority in conventional weapons. Pokhran II, therefore, only enhanced the status of Pakistan at India's detriment."[67] "To deal with the situation the party has urged the Government to Open talks with Pakistan for de-nuclearised environment in South Asia."[68]

The party claims that BJP's justification that nuclear tests would strengthen India's national security was merely a faulty prognosis. The party noted that after the tests, the contemplated strategic advantage that India was supposed to attain has dissipated like a hallucination, owing to the ground realities of the strategic equations of South Asia after Pakistan's nuclear response. The party had noted: "The one year since the Pokhran tests have amply shown the fallacy of this decision. India has not emerged stronger, but weakened by this adventurist policy. India found itself isolated internationally from its friends and the non-aligned community of nations. With the retaliatory tests conducted by Pakistan in Chagai, the two countries were set to enter into a nuclear arms race."[69]

Overall the party's views on the nuclear issue in Indo-Pakistan relations are based on the twin notions of anti-imperialism and anti-communalism. The party believes that the nuclearisation of the sub-continent is rooted in the communal factor and the implications of the process of nuclearisation symbolised that there is a return to a cold war paradigm marked by imperialist intervention at the cost of India's sovereignty. The party is much concerned with the economic repercussions of nuclear tests. It argued that to achieve a nuclear weapons status, the BJP led Government has accepted to surrender India's national interests to the imperialist USA.

Not only that, the party also has cited deviation of the post Pokhran foreign policy, from the fundamental principle of non-alignment. Finally, the party appears to have a pro-Chinese tilt. This was exhibited by the party's criticism of the BJP Government for naming China as the principal reason for carrying out nuclear tests. In this context the party noted: "The letter Vajpayee wrote in defence of Pokhran-II, to US president Clinton naming China as a country that possesses nuclear weapons and threatens India was an exaggerated threat perception at a time when for over a decade, the process of normalisation of relations with China was proceeding. Such a normalisation was in the interest of India for that reason successive Governments had pursued it. With this single unprovoked action, the Vajpayee Government had soured these relations."[70]

The approach of both the left parties to the nuclear question has been remarkably similar. The left has been the only group in the Indian political system that has come out strongly against nuclear weapons, even be it for the country's national security. Both condemned global nuclear regimes as symbols of neo-imperialism. The left also firmly believes that the machinations of the imperial U.S. have resulted in the nuclearisation of the sub-continent. It is in the light of this that we should visualise lefts position on the Indo-U.S. civilian nuclear deal. Since day one, it opposed the deal, merely to sustain its anti-American propaganda on the nuclear question but gradually moderation in its views is clearly visible.

Now it has accepted the Indo- U.S Civilian Nuclear deal but has warned the Indian Government not to shirk the path of an independent foreign policy under U.S. pressures and compromise India's national interest. The Communist parties have argued that the deal should be framed in such a way that it leads to an equal partnership between the two countries. Considerations of U.S. imperialism should not over determine India's strategic requirements. To this effect the left has acted as a potent pressure group that has considerably influenced India's stance on the nuclear deal and has made its presence felt at every stage of drawing the contours of the deal.

Attitude of various political parties on the nuclear question indicates the existence of substantial degree of consensus among the major Indian political parties. For instance, all the parties adhere to the long-held Indian principle of universal nuclear disarmament. They have in one voice, criticised the discriminatory global regimes, the NPT and CTBT.

Most significantly, all the political parties concur to the thesis that Pakistan's nuclear weaponisation has been Indo-centric because its national security paradigm is governed by its adversarial relations with India. Similarly they also correspond to the notion that Pakistan factor has been vital in determining India's policy response to the nuclear issues. Hence, almost all the parties appear to have a belief that the nuclear issue is an important component in the ambit of the bilateral relations between India and Pakistan.

But regarding China, it is only the BJP that has expressed security threat perceptions to India. In this regard, the Congress, the Janata Party and the Janata Dal, have displayed a sense of reticence. Anyway, the communist parties have severely criticised the BJP-led Government that it has exaggerated upon the China factor.

Pokhran-II nuclear test has been a significant event in the broad history of India. It provoked a unanimous opinion from almost all political parties except the left and they hailed it as a great technological breakthrough by Indian scientists. Anyhow, all the political parties criticised the BJP Government's timing of the test. They questioned the rational behind the tests and severely criticised the post-Pokhran II nuclear and foreign policy pursued by the BJP led coalition Government.

However, it is observed: "The attitudes of political parties cannot be termed as entirely unbiased. As considerations of party ideology and the underlying principles of the party structure, has a definitive impact."[71] For instance, the approach of the left towards nuclearisation of South Asia is considerably governed by its anti-imperialist ideological predilections and hence they have accented upon the American factor.

Further, "The opinions of political parties are oscillating in nature. Oscillating in the sense that they are subjected to changes by situational compulsions."[72] The approach of the Congress party to India's nuclear policy has been transformed from a position of pursuing a deliberate nuclear ambiguity to the maintainence of minimum credible nuclear weapons deterrence. This has happened due to Pakistan's nuclear weaponisation after Chagai, which has created a weaponised deterrence in South Asia. In this situation, to affect a roll back of India's policy of nuclear weaponisation is unimaginable. Simply due to the adverse consequences it may inflict upon India's national security.

In addition to this, political parties' position on nuclear disarmament reflects paradoxes. On the one hand, the parties call for a global approach for attaining the goal of universal nuclear disarmament, and except the left parties, no party has favoured a South Asian model of nuclear disarmament. But the threat perceptions of almost all political parties has been driven mainly by the Pakistan factor, that is their security threat perception has been galvanised by the factors active in India's neighbourhood.

Even the Chinese factor also has been accented by BJP in its approach to India's national security. But no party has cited any threat from the U.S., the U.K. or Russia. So, "When there is a grave security threat perception emanating from regional influences, will it not be judicious to evolve a regional model of nuclear disarmament or de-nuclearisation? Will it not be sagacious to initiate disarmament measures first within the region and then speak of universal disarmament? because charity begins at home."[73] Although Indian Governments be it of any party have persistently argued that India will not enter into any regional arrangement for nuclear disarmament, until the discriminatory nuclear regimes exist at the global level.

But it may be opined here that India can be a party to a regional mechanism that will facilitate the prevention of inadvertent or unauthorised use of nuclear weapons present in the region. India,China and Pakistan can arrive at a treaty of no first use and resolve to initiate confidence building measures to prevent nuclear accidents. This can be done without compromising India's long standing opposition to CTBT and NPT. This seems to be a very capricious suggestion. But if we consider the distant probability of the five established nuclear powers using their nuclear might against India, the idea may not be very impractical as long as it suits India's security interests in the region and evokes a sense of reciprocation and conformity on the part of our neighbours.

"It seems that political parties have not been able to evolve a consensus on a comprehensive nuclear policy for India. Though the draft nuclear doctrine has been proposed but it has been left languishing without any attempt to initiate a national level debate on the nature and implications of the doctrine. They have indulged only in mutual criticism, but have not come up with concrete policy options."[74] Hence the need of the hour is a national debate for bringing a common consensus on a firm and crystal clear nuclear policy for the country.

After a long time, Indian political parties have again, engaged themselves in a debate over the nuclear policy. This debate is expected to gain momentum in the coming days. On 16th December 2004, this debate was revitalised in the Rajya Sabha. The question of India's nuclear policy re-emerged on the national scene after former foreign minister in the UPA Government, Natwar Singh had remarked in an interview to a South Korean news paper that BJP led coalition Government had entered into a nuclear stand-off with Pakistan. Jaswant Singh present leader of the opposition in the Rajya Sabha expressed strong reservations over this statement. He contended: "Natwar Singh's statement had broken a tradition followed by successive Governments and taken our domestic policies to foreign shores. According to him, to say that the national democratic alliance Government had entered into a nuclear standoff with Pakistan belittled the totality of the country's nuclear programme."[75]

In the Rajya Sabha, replying to Jaswant Singh, the present Prime Minister Manmohan Singh maintained: "There is no uncertainty on the country's nuclear policy. India is a nuclear power and a responsible nuclear power."[76] Manmohan Singh had emphasised that Natvar Singh's remarks were merely a response to the queries posed by the journalists and it must not be conceived as a policy statement. Responding to Mr. Jaswant Singh's doubts on the continuity of the country's foreign policy, Manmohan Singh had asserted: "India's defence and foreign policy were decided on continuity and consent and need to be kept out of national politics."[77]

In the final analysis, it may be viewed that the renewed debate over India's nuclear policy has not gathered delightful momentum. A well-framed nuclear doctrine is today an urgent requirement in the interest of India's national security. A concerted and united endeavour on the part of all political parties transcending parochial considerations is desirable. Since the security environment of the sub-continent seems to be moving towards a position of weaponised deterrence and almost all the political parties in India approve this phenomenon, there should be little delay in formulating a comprehensive nuclear doctrine for the country.

## *References*


1. Ashwini K. Ray, Domestic politics and national security, *Economic and political weekly,* 33[26], June 1998, p.1631.
2. *Congress Marches Ahead,* January-February 1992, AICC publications, New Delhi, p.64.
3. K. Kamraj Nadar, Presidential address to the AICC meeting, Bhuvaneshwar, 1964, Congre*ss Presidential Speeches*, AICC Publication, New Delhi, 1975, p. 421.

4. George Perkovich, *India's nuclear bomb impact on global proliferation,* Oxford university press, New Delhi, 1999, p. 158.
5. *Indian National Congress,* Election Manifesto, general elections 1991, p. 54.
6. P.V.Narasimha Rao, Presidential address to the Congress Working Committee Meeting, 3rd June 1995, *Congress Marches Ahead,* 16th May 1993 31st December 1995, AICC publications, New Delhi, p. 156.
7. *Congress Marches Ahead,* January 1996 December 1997, AICC publications, New Delhi, p. 193.
8. *Congress Sandesh,* Monthly Journal of Indian National Congress, 1(10), August 1999, p. 1.
9. Indian National Congress, *Election Manifesto,* general elections 1996, p. 32.
10. K. Natwar Singh, *Congress Marches Ahead,* January 1998 – December 1998, AICC publications, New Delhi, p. 41.
11. Sonia Gandhi, *Congress Marches Ahead,* January 1998 – December 1998, AICC publications New Delhi, p. 23.
12. Indian national Congress *election manifesto,* general elections 2004.
13. Editorial of *Congress Sandesh,* 3(3), October 2000, p.4.
14. Ibid.
15. Pranab Mukherjee, *Congress Sandesh,* 1(11), September 1999, p. 34.
16. K. Natwar Singh, *Congress Marches Ahead,* January 1998 – December 1998, AICC publications, New Delhi, p. 39.
17. Madhav Rao Scindia, *Congress Sandesh,* 3(12), August 2001, p. 20.
18. *Congress Sandesh,* 2(1), October 1999, p. 17.
19. Indian National Congress, *Election Manifesto*, general elections 1999, p. 76.
20. *Security, Defence and Foreign Policy, The Congress Agenda,* AICC Publication, New Delhi, 2004, p. 11.
21. Indian national Congress, *resolution adopted at the 81st plenary session at Bangalore,* 2001, AICC publications, New Delhi, pp.34-38.
22. Indian national Congress, *Election manifesto,* general elections 1999, p.73.

23. George Perkovich, Supra No.4, p. 325.

24. Ibid., pp.151-152.

25. C. P. Thakur, Devendra P. Sharma, *India Under Atal Bihairi Vajpayee, The BJP Era,* UBS Publication, New Delhi, 1999, p. 132.

26. BJP *resolution adopted at the National Executive Meeting* at Cochin on April 23, 1981, in Foreign Policy Resolutions and Statements, 1980-1999, BJP secretariat New Delhi, pp.15-16.

27. Extract from the *Address by the party president L. K. Advani,* at the plenary session at Bombay on November 10-12, 1995, BJP secretariat, New Delhi.

28. L. K. Advani, *Presidential address,* National Council Session, Bangalore, 18th June 1993, President's addresses, L. K. Advani, 1986-1990, 1992-1998, BJP secretariat, New Delhi, 2000, p.122.

29. BJP national executive resolution, Supra, No. 26, p. 36.

30. Ibid., p. 9.

31. Extract from the address by the party president, L.K.Advani, Supra No 27, p. 57.

32. Bharatiya Janata Party, *Election Manifesto,* general elections, 1996, p. 37.

33. BJP *resolution adopted at the National Executive Meeting* held at Jaipur on August 21-23, 1998, BJP secretariat, New Delhi.

34. Ibid.

35. C. Rajamohan, *Crossing the rubicon: shaping of India's new foreign policy,* Penguin books, New Delhi, 2003, p.25.

36. A.B. Vajpayee, *Lok Sabha Debates,* (English version), 29th May 1998, Second Session (Twelfth Lok Sabha), Twelfth Series, II(3), Lok Sabha Secretariat, New Delhi, 1998, p. 388.

37. Amrita Abraham, First casualty is democracy, *Indian express*, 15 May 1998.

38. A.B. Vajpayee, Supra No. 36, p.388.

39. T. T. Poulose, India's nuclear option and national security, in P.R. Chari, Parvaiz Iqbal Cheema, Iftekhar Uzzaman ed, *nuclear non-proliferation in India and Pakistan: South Asian perspective,* Manohar publishers, New Delhi, 1996, p. 50.

40. *The Hindu*, September 4, 2003.

41. I. K. Gujral, *Lok Sabha Debates* (English version), second session Twelfth series, Twelfth Lok Sabha, 29 May 1998, Lok Sabha secretariat New Delhi 1998, pp. 347-348.

42. *The Hindu,* March 25, 1977.

43. *The Hindu,* May 16, 1977.

44. S. C. Gangal, Trends in India's Foreign Policy, in P.K.Misra (ed.), *Janata's Foreign Policy*, Vikas Publishing House, New Delhi, 1979, p. 54.

45. *Times of India,* 14 July 1977.

46. *Indian and Foreign Review,* 1st January 1978, p. 1.

47. S. C. Gangal, Supra, No. 44, p. 54.

48. Margaret Alva, *Janata's Foreign Policy : A Critique,* P.K.Misra, Ibid. p. 17.

49. P.R.Chari, *India's Nuclear Policy,* P. K. Misra, Ibid, pp. 60-61.

50. Janata Dal, *Election Manifesto 1998*, p. 18.

51. *Tribune,* 16th May 1998.

52. I. K. Gujral, *Lok Sabha Debates* (English version), September 11, 1996, Second Session (Eleventh Lok Sabha), Eleventh Series, 5(28), Lok Sabha Secretariat, New Delhi, 1996, p. 401.

53. H. D. Deve Gowda, *Times of India,* 16 May 1998.

54. I. K. Gujral, Supra, No. 41, p. 348.

55. Communist Party of India, *18th Party Congress Documents,* New Delhi, March 2002, CPI Publications, New Delhi, pp. 174-175.

56. Communist Party of India, *16th Party Congress Documents,* Thiruvanthapuram, October 1995, CPI Publications, New Delhi, pp. 37-38.

57. Communist party of India, *Election Manifesto,* general elections 1999, p. 2.

58. Communist Party of India, *Election Manifesto,* general elections, 2004, pp. 14-15.

59. Communist Party of India (Marxist), *15th Party Congress Documents,* Chandigarh, April 1995, CPI (M) Publications, New Delhi, p. 30.

60. Communist Party of India (Marxist), *Political Resolution adopted by 16th Congress,* October 1998, Calcutta, CPI (M) Publication, New Delhi, p. 33.

61. Communist Party of India (Marxist), *Election Manifesto,* General Election 1999, pp.4-5.

62. Harkishan Singh Surjeet, *People's Democracy,* CPI (M) Publication, 22(21), May 24, 1998, p. 1.

63. Ibid., p. 1.

64. Communist Party of India (Marxist) *Programme, updated by the party's Special Conference,* Thiruvananthapuram, October 2004, CPI (M) Publication, New Delhi, pp. 21-22.

65. Communist Party of India (Marxist), Political Resolution Supra No 60, p.33.

66. Communist Party of India (Marxist), *Political Resolution adopted at the 17th Congress,* Hyderabad, March 2002, CPI (M) Publication, New Delhi, p. 25.

67. Communist Party of India (Marxist), *13+4 Months of BJP Misrule,* CPI (M) Publication, New Delhi, 1999, p. 8.

68. Communist Party of India (Marxist), *Election Manifesto,* General Election 2004, p. 17.

69. *People's Democracy,* CPI (M) Publication, 23(20), May 16, 1999, p. 1.

70. Communist Party of India (Marxist), Supra, No. 67, p. 8.

71. *Author's Interview* with Muchkund Dubey former Foreign Secretary, 20th September 2004, Panjim, Goa.

72. *Author's Interview* with C. Raja Mohan, Strategic affairs editor, Indian express, 19th September 2004, Panjim, Goa.

73. Ibid.

74. Author's Interview, Supra, No. 71

75. *The Hindu,* 17th December 2004.

76. Ibid.

77. Ibid.

## Chapter 10

# An Evaluation

"Pakistan factor has been a dominant proposition that has determined the nature of India's foreign policy and molded its national security paradigm."[1] India has been embroiled in the politics of South Asia and its role in world affairs has been encumbered due to the unresolved Indo-Pakistan conflict. Since independence, India's foreign policy makers have made unrelenting endeavours to find amicable solutions to this conundrum, but the desired results appear to be a reverie.

With an ever increasing terrorist violence and failure of the two Governments to identify concrete measures to deal with the menace, the dispute always seem to amplify and prognosticates the worse to come. The Indo-Pakistan equations appear to be advancing into a "Clash of civilizations syndrome."[2] With our policy makers stranded without any answer to cross border terrorism. The joint anti-terrorism mechanism mooted in the recent meeting of the leaders of India and Pakistan at Havana, has already been dubbed as obscure and unworkable. The BJP has termed it as one of the biggest foreign policy gamble of the Manmohan Singh Government.

When the world is moving in the direction of integration through globalization, where political disputes are being compromised for economic progress. Compelling Francis Fukuyama to declare that there is "End of history:"[3] denoting that the world is progressing towards liberal democracy or what David Held calls "A Cosmopolitan Democracy."[4] But India and Pakistan appear to be a throw back incapable of adaptability to these radical transformations. The politics of the sub-continent seem to be retrograding, with each new terrorist strikes forcing them one step behind.

The cold war has ended, signaling the termination of ideological confrontation, or as Danial Bell had contemplated the demise of the role of ideology in political affairs in his famous thesis of the "End of ideology".[5] The same has been indicated by the unification of Germany and creation of the European Union but Indo-Pakistan confrontation illustrates a reincarnation of the cold war paradigm and it appears that the epicenter has shifted from Europe and America to South Asia. The two countries still seem to be enmeshed in an ideological dispute, signifying the Kashmir dispute as the epitome of a struggle between two anti-thetical ideologies secularism as professed by India and the two nation theory, advocated by Pakistan.

Hence until Indo-Pakistan relations do not witness a qualitative transformation from an intense belligerence to a broad based and unbiased co-operation. As long as ephemeral solutions are euphemistically advocated by the leaders on both sides as remedies, Indo-Pakistan conflict is bound to remain kindled. Thus the Pakistan factor which has endured as a vital component of India's foreign policy and national security paradigm will continue to remain in the same position engrossing thoughts and actions of the foreign policy makers.

Nearly six decades have rolled by, bilateral relations of India and Pakistan seems to be mired in history. The tides of changes may have occurred in the socio-economic field but does not seem to effect their political relations. The two countries have fought four wars and signed many agreements, but it appears that the sub-continent is in a state of inertia.

Even when three open wars could not decide the future of the sub-continent and failed to metamorphosise the environment. Proxy war and cross-border terrorism have engulfed the fate of millions in the region. The mistrust and animosity has reached the hilt when the sub-continental affairs assumed a nuclear dimension, resulting in Kashmir acquiring a critical posture, with the growing international recognition that the region is emerging as a nuclear flash point.

All these points to a comprehensive study of Indo-Pakistan relations from the perspective of key issues like Kashmir issue and the nuclear question, harmonious relations between the two countries may be a probability only if these problems are effectively tackled. The foreign policies of the two countries are mainly directed towards sorting out the disputes between the two countries with a genuine commitment. But due to this the efficiency of foreign policy to deal with other international affairs seems to have debilitated. Anyhow, foreign policy question and national security interests in India and Pakistan have been viewed from the prism of their bilateral relations.

Domestic space in both countries has been occupied by the issues pertaining to their mutual relations. In view of this, internal variables have played a significant part in determining their foreign policies towards each other. In India, political parties being the key institutional mechanisms which operatise the democratic setup and also have given an institutional character to public opinion by acting as a bridge between people and foreign policy makers have played a significant part in the shaping of India's policy response towards Pakistan.

They have given adequate priority to the issues of Indo-Pakistan relations. In their pronouncements regarding foreign policy articulated in their programmes, policies, agenda, election manifestoes and resolutions. Irrespective of their ideological predilections, political parties in India consider Indo-Pakistan relations as one of the major challenge confronted by India's foreign policy and they believe that the success of India's security strategy considerably depends upon its capability to maintain peaceful relations with Pakistan.

In this context the ruling party on the basis of its policy pronouncements and perceptions on various issues formulates tangible policies to skillfully tackle the problem of Indo-Pakistan relations. In the same way, opposition parties seem to have backed the Government in its endeavour of searching an amicable solution to Indo-Pakistan problems. They not only caution the Government by their criticism if the Government is not effective, but they also give their policy prescriptions on the basis of their understanding of international situation.

This indicates that national consensus has been the key foundation of India's Pakistan policy. But this consensus is not coherent and appears to be incongruous. Although the approach of political parties have reflected the existence of a broad consensus, on acute issues of Indo-Pakistan relations such as the nature of Kashmir dispute, impact of cross border terrorism on the security situation and the implications of the nuclear factor. But on these matters political parties differ among themselves on various aspects which lead to the emergence of a consensus that is distorted and obscure.

In India it has been identified that the gulf of separation has not existed only between the ruling party and the opposition, but each and every party attempts to assert its independent identity. This may lead to divergent perceptions regarding an issue, resulting in their diametric policy prescription. It means that even in a coalition Government the policy outlook of all the political parties which are parts of the Government, may not be uniform. This happens because: "The constituent units of a coalition do not tend to lose their separate entity."[6]

The primary reason for this may be that every party differs from each other, as they have different histories, social support base, principles underlying their party organization and most significantly the ideology that forms its bedrock.

Hence due to the multifarious character of the Indian society a multi party system was established. Thaw in the one party dominant system, resulted in the emergence of the era of coalition Governments. The dominant character of such a system is that each party represents different groups of the society, they have different outlook on significant policy issues relating to Pakistan affairs. Bhartiya Janta Party headed coalition Governments consecutively for six years and an assessment of the responses of some of its constituent units to various policy initiatives of the Government pertaining to Pakistan, demonstrates clear political eccentricity.

For instance, the Vajpayee Government in its bid to normalise relations with Pakistan decided to declare a unilateral ceasefire in Jammu&Kashmir. Although it got a positive response from the opposition parties, but what was uncanonical was that BJP's own ally the Shivasena, firmly contested the move. "Vajpayee's task was to tell Pakistan in particular and the world in general that even though he headed a coalition Government whose main constituent he himself represented, the BJP the Hindu rightist party which perused a sectarian agenda. India's policy remains one of co-operative friendship with its neighbours, with which it had bitter relations marked by frictions, conflict and war during the last fifty years. While carrying this onerous task, Vajpayee left no one in doubt about the sincerity of his intensions. It would be the height of cynicism, to call this pronouncement as symbolism or empty rhetoric or gimmickry."[7]

But "In an embarrassment to the NDA Government, its ally Shivasena staged a walk out in the Lok Sabha, over the Governments announcement of the unilateral ceasefire."[8] This exhibits chasm among the approaches of different political parties. Inspite of being the part of the Government, a party may reflect a deviant attitude to a policy initiative. Hence it has been viewed: "Political parties form alliances, without least regard for policy issues."[9]

With this background, if we examine the role of political parties in the shaping of India's policies towards Pakistan, the following observations can be made.

Regarding the centrality of the Kashmir issue in Indo-Pakistan conflict all parties depict concensus and they are united on the notion that normalisation of Indo-Pakistan relations presupposes the amicable solution to the Kashmir issue. But when it comes to identifying the primary causes for the discord, various political parties have expressed divergences. If the BJP condemned the Congress for enacting article 370 that gave special status to Jammu&Kashmir and argued that it led to the weakening of vigil on the State by the centre that facilitated Pakistan to interfere and indulge in machinations with extremist forces within the State. Contrary to this the Congress has accused that the non-Congress Governments' internal security strategies have been weak and the socio-economic policies in Kashmir were marked by a lack of vision that has led to the alienation of people of Jammu&Kashmir and ushered in with the liberation movement and this internal destabilisation has been exploited by the Pakistani strategists for their own advantage.

The left takes a very different position. It has criticised the imperialist machinations of the U.S. which was instrumental in pushing Kashmir into the cold war grand strategy and led to the outbreak of the present situation. For this, the Communist parties have held the subsequent Indian Governments responsible and condemned them of reflecting a pro-American tilt and alleged them of yielding to American pressures. These differences among political parties have not only brought divergent perspectives to the Kashmir issue, but has also resulted in the policy prescriptions of various political parties to be diverse.

Concerning the nuclear factor, political parties inspite of having unanimity of opinion regarding the threats to India's security in the neighbourhood, have diverse opinions on the question of the use of the nuclear option. The BJP insisted firmly that India should weaponise its nuclear capacity owing to the perilous security situation in the region. contrary to this the Congress, the Janata party and the Janata Dal, favoured a policy of deliberate nuclear ambiguity.

The left however has expressed a profound antipathy to the idea of weaponising the defence mechanism and it has firmly maintained this position even after India's changed nuclear status after 1998. The CPI[M] expressed its post Pokhran II position "Against the induction of nuclear weapons."[10] Similarly, the CPI said, "now that India has demonstrated its nuclear capability, there should be no attempt to induct nuclear weapons into our strategic or tactical arsenal."[11] Such discrepancies in the outlook of political parties to key issues influencing the matrix of India Pakistan relations has obfuscated the situation and distorted the concensus on India's policies towards Pakistan.

Thus an examination of the role of Indian political parties in the shaping of the nations policy towards Pakistan, indicates that their role has not been very significant in neither interpreting the problems, nor in exploring feasible solutions to deal with this vexed issue. This has happened not because they do not have a consensus on the nature and gravity of the problem, but they tend to view it from different perspectives. Unfortunately, they have also attempted to politicise the issues of Indo-Pakistan relations in order to gain political capital.

In an urge to achieve mileage over their political opponents, parties have interpreted and criticised India's policies towards Pakistan in a manner that would suit their own requirements. Although they may have evinced considerable interest in the affairs relating to Pakistan, their position has been oscillating, that is, it has tended to vacillate according to their position in the political system and considerations of party ideology. In other words, their perceptions change according to the nature of their role; holding Governmental office or sitting in the opposition.

For example, they seem to be very critical regarding an issue, while they are in opposition. But when they come to power, they appear to moderate their stance and follow the same policy by accepting the ground realities and coming to terms with the domestic compulsions and the turbulence of world politics. In this context it may be noted that the BJP which adopted a very critical posture towards management of India-Pakistan relations and made radical suggestions in this regard, considerably moderated its stance after it came to power.

The two wings within the party the hardliners and the moderates have stood diametrically opposed to each other when it comes to defining the party's position on issues of India-Pakistan relations. As an opposition, the party had demonstrated extremist approach while suggesting solution to the Kashmir issue and this indicates that the party's agenda in its earlier days was dictated by the hardliners. But when it came to power, its approach to the Kashmir conflict transformed drastically. The diplomatic initiatives such as the Lahore process and the Srinagar peace offer provide credence to this argument. Hence it can be deduced that the role of the hardliners in determining BJP Government's foreign policy considerably diluted.

Hence, the role of the opposition is crucial; it should not criticise a particular policy without proper comprehension of the facts determining a phenomenon. Their role in this regard must be creative, unbiased and above partisan interests. Considerations of national interest should over determine calculations of vote bank politics and concerns of power politics.

Apart from this, political parties lack intra-party democracy. A large number of members do not get ample opportunity to express their views on a foreign policy issue like Indo-Pakistan relations. One of the significant reasons for this is that every political party has a coterie which is its think tank and it is identified with a particular leader and that leader's views are reflected as the stand of the party.

Further, in party meetings, discussions are not held formally on issues concerning Indo-Pakistan relations. Only resolutions are being adopted mechanically without sufficient rumination. Hence, political parties have a responsibility of educating and training their members on foreign policy matters and provide them with ample opportunity to express their views. In order to engage them more effectively in formulating the party's foreign policy resolutions to ensure their wider participation in the process of formulation of India's foreign policy.

By and large, it has been found that political parties do not meaningfully discuss and debate the issues and problems of Indo-Pakistan relations in the parliament. Primarily, due to the large number of parties and shortage of time in the parliament, each and every party may not get sufficient time to express its opinion. Besides, parliament's time is wasted due to disruption and walkouts.

Thus the foreign policy initiatives for dealing with problems of Indo-Pakistan relations seem to be formally accepted or criticised by the members of different political parties without comprehensive discussion.

To conclude, it may be viewed that despite these serious incongruities, the role of political parties in democratising the foreign policy making mechanism, in spite of divergent perceptions, cannot be undermined. They have institutionalised public opinion in a large and diverse nation like India, through the process of interest articulation and interest aggregation. By this they create a vital link between the citizens and the foreign policy makers. This has facilitated the sustenance of liberal democracy in India. When we witness frequent destabilisation of the democratic regimes in our neighbourhood, the crucial role of political parties in the process of policy formulation, seems to have gained wider recognition. Although the political interests of the parties are diametrically opposed to each other, these divergences have not grievously jeopardised India's national interest.

## *References*

1. Rajpal Budania, *India's national security dilemma The Pakistan factor and India's policy response,* Indus, New Delhi, 2001.
2. Samuel P. Huntington, *Clash of civilisations and the remaking*

*of the new world order*, Simon and Schuster, London, 1998.

3. Francis, Fukuyama, *End of history and the last man*, Penguin Books, London, 1993.
4. David Held ed., *Prospects for democracy*, Stanford University Press, Stanford California, 1993, p.13.
5. Daniel Bell, *The end of ideology*, The free press, New York, 1962.
6. David L. Sills ed., *International Encyclopedia of Social-Sciences,* 1968, p.533.
7. Poonam Singh and Ira Yadav, Bus trip to Lahore, a harbinger of Indo-Pakistan co-operation in the coming Millennium, *Review of Politics* 7[2] 1999, p.55.
8. *Pioneer,* 25 November 2000.
9. Sudha Pai, The Indian party system under transformation: Lok Sabha 1998, *Asian Survey,* 38[9] September 1998, p.844.
10. *13+4 months of BJP misrule, No.5 Pokhran to Kargil*, CPI[M] publications New Delhi 1999, pp. 6-7.
11. *Hindustan Times,* 16 May 1998.

# Select Bibliography


**Primary Sources**

**Party Documents, Indian National Congress**

*Congress Marches Ahead*, 16th May 1993, - 31st December 1995, AICC Publication, New Delhi.

*Congress Marches Ahead*, January 1992 - February 1993, AICC Publication, New Delhi.

*Congress Marches Ahead*, January 1996 – December 1997, AICC Publication, New Delhi.

*Congress Marches Ahead*, January 1998 – December 1998, AICC Publication, New Delhi.

*Congress Marches Ahead*, March 1, 1993 – May 15, 1993, AICC Publication, New Delhi.

Congress, *Shimla Sankalp*, Shimla, 7-9 July 2003, AICC Publication, New Delhi.

Indian National Congress, *Resolution adopted at the 81st Plenary Session,* Bangalore, 2001, AICC Publication, New Delhi.

Indian National Congress, *Security, Defence and Foreign Policy, The Congress Agenda,* AICC Publication, New Delhi.

Indian National Congress, *Text of Resolutions adopted at the 80th Plenary Session,* Calcutta, 1997, AICC Publication, New Delhi.

*Resolutions adopted at the All India Congress Committee Meeting,* New Delhi, 24th May 2002, AICC Publication.

*Resolutions adopted at the All India Congress Committee Meeting,* New Delhi, 25th May 1999, AICC Publication.

**Election Manifesto of Indian National Congress**

Indian National Congress, *Election Manifesto* 1991, AICC Publication, New Delhi.

Indian National Congress, *Election Manifesto* 1996, AICC Publication, New Delhi.

Indian National Congress, *Election Manifesto* 1998, AICC Publication, New Delhi.

Indian National Congress, *Election Manifesto* 1999, AICC Publication, New Delhi.

Indian National Congress, *Election Manifesto* 2004, AICC Publication, New Delhi.

Indian National Congress, *Congress Sandesh,* A Monthly Journal of Indian National Congress, AICC Publication, New Delhi.

**Bharatiya Janata Party**

Bharatiya Janata Party. *Foreign Policy Resolutions and Statements 1980-1999,* BJP Publication, New Delhi.

Bharatiya Janata Party, *Political Resolutions, 1980-1999,* BJP Publication, New Delhi.

Bharatiya Janata Party, *Resolutions adopted by National Executive Council,* 72-28 August 2002, Nagpur, BJP Publication, New Delhi.

Bharatiya Janata Party, *Resolutions adopted by the National Executive Meeting,* 29 December 2001, New Delhi, BJP Publication, New Delhi.

Bharatiya Janata Party, *Resolutions adopted by National Executive Meeting,* 12-14 April 2002, Panaji, BJP Publication, New Delhi.

Bharatiya Janata Party, *President's Addresses* by Dr. Murli Manohar Joshi, 1991-1993, BJP Publication, New Delhi.

Bharatiya Janata Party, *President's Address* by L. K. Advani, 1986-1990, 1993-98, BJP Publication, New Delhi.

Bharatiya Janata Party, Prime Minister, A.B.Vajpayee, *Selected Speeches*, Vol. 1, March 1998 to March 1999, BJP Publication, New Delhi.

Bharatiya Janata Party, Prime Minister, A.B.Vajpayee, *Selected Speeches*, Vol. II, April 1999 to March 2000, BJP Publication, New Delhi.

Bharatiya Janata Party, *Vision Document*, issued on the occasion of elections to the 14th Lok Sabha, May 2004, BJP Publication, New Delhi.

Bharatiya Janata Party, *Stability, Prosperity*, Global Prestige, Good Governance, Achievements of NDA Government, BJP Publication, New Delhi, 2004

Bharatiya Janata Party, *Election Manifesto*, 1991, BJP Publication, New Delhi.

Bharatiya Janata Party, *Election Manifesto*, 1996, BJP Publication, New Delhi.

Bharatiya Janata Party, *Election Manifesto*, 1998, BJP Publication, New Delhi.

Bharatiya Janata Party, *Election Manifesto*, 1999, BJP Publication, New Delhi.

Bharatiya Janata Party, *Election Manifesto*, 2004, BJP Publication, New Delhi.

Bharatiya Janata Party, *BJP Today*, A Fortnightly Journal of Bharatiya Janata Party, BJP Publication, New Delhi.

**Janata Dal**

Janata Dal, V. P.Singh, Social Justice for Secular India, *Selected Speeches*, Janata Dal Publication, New Delhi, 1990.

Janata Dal, *Election Manifesto,* 1998, Janata Dal Publication, New Delhi.

**Communist Party of India (CPI)**

Communist Party India, *16th Congress Documents,* New Delhi, October 1995, CPI Publication, New Delhi.

Communist Party of India, *18th Party Congress Documents,* Thiruvananthapuram, March 26-31, 2002, CPI Publication, New Delhi.

Communist Party of India, *Political Organizational Report* adopted by the National Council Meeting, New Delhi, 11-13 May 2003, CPI Publication, New Delhi.

Communist Party of India, *Election Manifesto,* 1991, CPI Publication, New Delhi.

Communist Party of India, *Election Manifesto,* 1996, CPI Publication, New Delhi.

Communist Party of India, *Election Manifesto,* 1998, CPI Publication, New Delhi.

Communist Party of India, *Election Manifesto,* 1999, CPI Publication, New Delhi.

Communist Party of India, *Election Manifesto*, 2004, CPI Publication, New Delhi.

**Communist Party of India (Marxist)**

Communist Party of India (Marxist), *Documents of the 15th Congress of the Communist Party of India (Marxist),* Chandigarh, April 3-8, 1995, CPI (M) Publication, New Delhi.

Communist Party of India (Marxist), *Political Organizational Report,* adopted by 16th Congress of CPI (M), 5-11 October 1998, Calcutta, CPI (M) Publication, New Delhi.

Communist Party of India (Marxist), *Programme updated by the Special Conference of CPI (M),* Thiruvananthapuram, October 20-23, 2000, CPI (M) Publication, New Delhi.

Communist Party of India (Marxist), *17th Congress Documents,* adopted by 17th Congress of CPI (M), Hyderabad, 19-24 March 2002, CPI (M) Publication, New Delhi.

Communist Party of India (Marxist), *Report on Current Developments,* adopted at the Central Committee Meeting held on September 28-30, 2003, New Delhi, CPI (M) Publication, New Delhi.

Communist Party of India (Marxist), *Report on Current Development,* adopted at the Central Committee Meeting held between January 29 and 31, 2004, at Hyderabad, CPI (M) Publication, New Delhi.

Communist Party of India (Marxist), *13+4 Months of BJP Misrule,* published on the occasion of General Elections 1999, CPI (M) Publication, New Delhi.

Communist Party of India (Marxist), *Election Manifesto,* 1991, CPI (M) Publication, New Delhi.

Communist Party of India (Marxist), *Election Manifesto,* 1996, CPI (M) Publication, New Delhi.

Communist Party of India (Marxist), *Election Manifesto,* 1998, CPI (M) Publication, New Delhi.

Communist Party of India (Marxist), *Election Manifesto,* 1999, CPI (M) Publication, New Delhi.

Communist Party of India (Marxist), *Election Manifesto,* 2004, CPI (M) Publication, New Delhi.

Communist Party of India (Marxist), *People's Democracy,* Weekly Organ of the CPI (M).

Singh, Harkishan Surjeet, *BJP exposed, no more of this Government,* CPI (M) Publication, New Delhi.

**Lok Sabha Debates**

Advani, L. K., *Lok Sabha Debates,* Thirteenth Series, 3(13), Lok Sabha, Secretariat, New Delhi, December 15, 1999.

Gujral, I. K., *Lok Sabha Debates* Series, 2(21), Lok Sabha, Secretariat, New Delhi, March 20, 1997.

Gujral, I.K., *Lok Sabha Debates* (English Version), 29th May 1998, Second Session (Twelfth Lok Sabha), Twelfth Series, 2(3), Lok Sabha, Secretariat, New Delhi, 1998.

Gujral, I.K., *Lok Sabha Debates* (English Version), September 11, 1996, Second Session (Eleventh Lok Sabha), Eleventh Series, 5(28), Lok Sabha, Secretariat, New Delhi, 1998.

Khurana, Madan Lal, *Lok Sabha Debates,* Seventh Session, Thirteenth Lok Sabha, 18(13), Lok Sabha, Secretariat, New Delhi, August 8, 2001.

Reddy, Jaipal, *Lok Sabha Debates,* Seventh Session, Thirteenth Lok Sabha, 18(13), Lok Sabha, Secretariat, New Delhi, August 8, 2001.

Singh, Jaswanth, *Lok Sabha Debates,* Third Session, Eleventh Lok Sabha, Vol. 6, Lok Sabha, Secretariat, New Delhi, December 4, 1996.

Vaiko, *Lok Sabha Debates* (English Version), 29th May 1998, Second Session, (Twelfth Lok Sabha), Twelfth Series, 2(3), Lok Sabha, Secretariat, New Delhi, 1998.

Vajpayee, Atal Behari, *Lok Sabha Debates* (English Version), 29th May 1998, Second Session (Twelfth Lok Sabha), Twelfth Series, 2(3), Lok Sabha, Secretariat, New Delhi, 1998.

Vajpayee, Atal Behari, *Lok Sabha Debates,* Twelfth Series, 2(9), Twelfth Lok Sabha, Lok Sabha, Secretariat, New Delhi, June 8, 1998.

**Rajya Sabha Debates**

Deve Gowda, H.D., *Rajya Sabha Debates,* 178(17), Rajya Sabha Secretariat, New Delhi, 2 August 1996.

Jagmohan, *Rajya Sabha Debates,* 175(3), Rajya Sabha Secretariat, New Delhi, 29 November 1995.

Singh, Manmohan, *Rajya Sabha Debates,* 19(4), Rajya Sabha Secretariat, New Delhi, 23 November 2000.

Vayalar Ravi, *Rajya Sabha Debates,* 175(31), Rajya Sabha Secretariat, New Delhi, 29 November, 1995.

## Secondary Sources

### Books

Ahmed, Aziz, *Islamic Culture in Indian Environment,* Oxford University Press, New Delhi, 1999.

Ambedkar, B.R., *Pakistan and Partition of India,* Thacker Publications, Bombay, 1945.

Ayub, Mohammad, *India, Pakistan and Bangladesh : Search for New Relationship,* Indian Council of World Publication, New Delhi, 1975.

Bahadur, Kalim, *Democracy in Pakistan – Crisis and Conflicts,* Har-Anand Publications, New Delhi, 1998.

Bandhyopadhyaya, J., *The Making of India's Foreign Policy,* Allied Publishers, New Delhi, 1991.

Barnds, William J., *India, Pakistan and the Great Powers,* Pall Mall Press, London, 1972.

Baxter, Craig, *Jana Sangh : Biography of an Indian Political Party,* Oxford University Press, Bombay, 1972.

Budania, Rajpal, *India's National Security Dilemma* The Pakistan Factor and India's Policy Response, Indus, New Delhi, 2001.

Bhutto, Zulfiquar Ali, *The Myth of Independence,* Oxford University Press, Lahore, 1969.

Blinkenberg, Lars, *India-Pakistan : The History of Unsolved Conflicts,* An Analysis of Some Structural Factors, Odense University Press, Odense, 2001.

Burke, S. M. and Ziring Lawrence, *Pakistan's Foreign Policy : A Historical Analysis,* Oxford University Press, Karachi, 1990.

Burke, S. M., *Mainsprings of Indian and Pakistani Foreign Policies*, University of Minnesota Press, Minneapolis, 1974.

Chari, P.R., *Indo-Pak Nuclear Standoff – The Role of the United States,* Manohar Publication, New Delhi, 1995.

Chari, P.R., Parvaiz, Iqbal Cheema, and Iftekharuzzaman, (ed.), *Nuclear Non-Proliferation in India and Pakistan – South Asian Perspectives,* Manohar Publication, New Delhi, 1996.

Cohen, Stephen, P. *Perceptions, Influence and Weapons Proliferation in South Asia,* Occasional Paper 1, Office of Arms Control, Disarmament and International Security, University of Illinois, August 1979.

Colonel, Ravi Nanda, AVSM, *Indo-Pak Detente*, Lancers, New Delhi, 1989.

Colonel, Ravi Nanda, AVSM, *Kashmir and Indo-Pak Relations,* Lancer's Books, New Delhi, 2001.

Dixit, J. N., *India and Pakistan in War and Peace*, India Today Group, New Delhi, 2002.

Dixit, J.N., *Anatomy of a Flawed Inheritance,* Konark, New Delhi, 1995.

Dutta, V.P., *India's Foreign Policy,* Vikas Publishing House, New Delhi, 1984.

Fisher, David, *Stopping the Spread of Nuclear Weapons : The Post and the Prospects,* Routledge, London, 1992.

Frankel, Joseph, *The Making of Foreign Policy : An Analysis of Decision Making,* Oxford University Press London 1973.

Ganguly, Sumit, *Conflict Unending, India-Pakistan Tensions Since 1947,* Oxford University Press, New Delhi, 2002.

George, Perkovich, *India's Nuclear Bomb : The Impact on Global Proliferation,* Oxford University Press, New Delhi, 1999.

Ghosh, Ajoy, *Indo-Pak Conflict – Threat to South Asian Security,* Reference Press Publication, New Delhi, 2003.

Gupta, Sisir, *Kashmir : A Study in Indo-Pakistan Relations,* Asia Publishing House, Bombay, 1966.

Hagerty, Devin, *The Consequences of Nuclear Proliferation : Lessons from South Asia,* MIT Press, Cambridge, 1998.

Hartmann, Frédric H., *The Relations of Nations,* Macmilan, New York, 1978.

Hassan, Mushirul, *Introduction to India's Partition Process : Strategy and Mobilisation,* Oxford University Press, New Delhi, 1997.

Hassan, Sarwar K. (ed.), *The Kashmir Question Documents on the Foreign Relations of Pakistan,* Institution of International Affairs, Karachi, 1966.

Hudson, H.V., *The Great Divide,* Hutchinson, London, 1969.

Jaisingh, Hari, *Kashmir a Tale of Shame,* UBS Publications, New Delhi, 1996.

Jalal, Ayesha, *The State of Martial Rule : The Origin of Pakistani Political Economy of Defence,* Cambridge University Press, Cambridge, 1990.

Jayaramu, P.S., *India's National Security and Foreign Policy,* ABC Publication, New Delhi, 1987.

John, L. Esposito and John O. Voll, *Islam and Democracy,* Oxford University Press, Oxford, 1996.

Kavic, Lorne J., *India's Quest for Security,* University of California Press, Berkeley, 1967.

Khan, Mohammed Ayub, *Friends Not Masters,* Oxford University Press, London, 1966.

Kishor, Mohammed Ali, *Jana Sangh and India's Foreign Policy,* Associated Publishing House, New Delhi, 1969.

Korbel, Joseph, *Danger in Kashmir,* Princeton University Press, Princeton, 1954.

Krosney, Herbert, and Weisman, Steve, *The Islamic Bomb,* Times Books, New York, 1981.

Lefever, Ernest, W., *Nuclear Arms in the Third World : US Policy Dilemma,* The Bookings Institution, Washington, 1979.

Mary, Doreen Wainwright and Philips, C.H., (ed.), *The Partition of India : Policies and Perspectives,* Allen and Unwin, London, 1975.

Patagundi, S.S., *India's Foreign Policy : An Elitist Perception,* Uppal Publishing House, New Delhi, 1995.

Paul, T.V., *Asymmetric Conflicts: War Initiation by Weaker Powers,* Cambridge University Press, Cambridge, 1994.

Pillai, K. Raman, *India's Foreign Policy : Basic Issues and Political Attitudes,* Meenakshi Publications, Meerut, 1964.

Prakash and Shah, Ghulam Mohammad, (ed.), *Towards Understanding the Kashmir Crisis,* Gyan Publishing House, New Delhi, 2002.

Prasad, Bimal, (ed.), *India's Foreign Policy: Studies in Continuity and Change,* Vikas Publishing House, New Delhi, 1979.

Puri, Geet, *Bharatiya Jana Sangh: Organisation and Ideology,* Sterling Publishers, New Delhi, 1980.

Raj Changappa, *Weapons of Peace: The Secret Story of India's Quest to Be a Nuclear Power*, Harper Collins, New Delhi, 2000.

Ray, Aswini, K., *Domestic Compulsions and Foreign Policy,*

*Pakistan in Indo-Soviet Relations 1947-1958,* Manas Publications, New Delhi, 1975.

Sartori, Giovanni, *Parties and Party System : A Framework for Analysis,* Vol. 1, Cambridge University Press, London, 1976.

Sattar, Abdul, *Reducing Nuclear Dangers in South Asia,* Institute of Regional Studies, Islamabad, November 1994.

Sawnny, Karan R., (ed.), *Kashmir How Far can Vajpayee and Musharraf Go ?*, Peace Publication, New Delhi, 2001.

Sinha, P. B., and Subramanian, R.R., *Nuclear Pakistan : Atomic Threat to South Asia,* Vision Books, New Delhi, 1980.

Sir Moon, Penderel, *Divide and Quit,* Oxford University Press, New Delhi, 1998.

Spector, Leonard, S. and Smith, Jacqueliner, *Nuclear Ambitions : The Spread of Nuclear Weapons 1989-90,* West View Press, Boulder, 1990.

Sundarji, K., *Blind Men of Hindustan and Pakistan Indo-Pak Nuclear War,* UBS Publishers, New Delhi, 1993.

Vajpayee, A.B., *New Dimensions of India's Foreign Policy,* Vision Books, New Delhi, 1979.

Wirsing, Roberg G., *India Pakistan and the Kashmir Dispute,* Rupa and Company, New Delhi, 1994.

Zaidi, Moin A., *Annual Register of Indian Political Parties, Proceedings and Fundamental Texts 1973-1974,* Indian Institute of Applied Political Research, New Delhi, 1974.

**Articles**

Ahmed, Samina, Cortrigh, David and Matto Amitabh, Public Opinion and Nuclear Options for South Asia, *Asian Survey,* 38(8), August 1998.

Ahmed, Samina, Pakistan's Nuclear Weapons Programme : Turning Point and Nuclear Choices, *International Security,* 23(4), Spring 1999.

Alavi, Hamza, Social Forces and Ideology in the Making of Pakistan, *Economic and Political Weekly,* 37(51), December 21, 2002.

Bahadur, Kalim, India and Pakistan Relations in 21st Century, *World Focus,* 226-227, 1998.

Banerjee, Subrata, Politics of BJP's Nuclear Weapon Strategy, *New Age,* 46(27), 5 July 1998.

Bhargava, G.S., Kashmir Ceasefire General Musharraf's Stake, *Mainstream,* 39(9), February 17, 2001.

Bhattacharya, Purushottam, Nuclear Policy of the Vajpayee Government: *A Journey into Nowhere, Mainstream,* 36(19), 2 May 1998.

Bidanda, M. Chengappa, Pakistan Insight into Islamization, *Strategic Analysis,* 22(10), January 1999.

Bose, Sumantra, Kashmir: Sources of Conflict, Dimensions of Peace, *Economic and Political Weekly,* 34(13), March 27, 1999.

Choudhary, C.K., Cross-Border Terrorism : Pakistan's Compulsions, *Constraints and Stakes, India Quarterly,* 57(2), April-June 2001.

Daruwalla, K.N., Pakistan: State, Policy and the ISI, *USI Journal,* (India's Oldest Journal on Defence Affairs), 130(539), January-March 2000.

Datta, V. N., Iqbal, Jinnah and India's Partition – An Intimate Relationship, *Economic and Political Weekly,* 37(50), December 14, 2002.

Dixit, Abha, Indo-Pak Relations Today, *World Focus,* 222-223, June-July 1998.

Dubey, Muchkund, For a Broad Based Dialogue with the

Kashmiri People, *Mainstream,* 29(10), February 24, 2001.

Dubey, Muchkund, World Nuclear Order and India's Deterrence, *Mainstream,* 36(27), 27 June 1998.

Evans, Alexander, Talibanising Kashmir, *The World Today,* 57(12), December 2001.

Fessica, Stern, Pakistan's Jihad Culture, *Foreign Affairs,* 79(6), July/August 2000.

Gregory, Shaun, A Formidable Challenge : Nuclear Command and Control in South Asia, *Disarmament Diplomacy,* 54 February 2001.

Gupta, Bhabani Sen, Vajpayee's Foreign Policy: Who to Engage and Who Not to, *Mainstream,* 37(47), 13 November 1999.

Hilati, A.S., Kashmir: Emerging Nuclear Threat in South Asian Perspectives, *The Central European Review of International Affairs,* Summer 2001.

Jagmohan, Nuclear Testing, Kashmir and the United States, *Organiser,* 50(2), 9 August 1998.

Kanwal, Gurmeet, Proxy War in Kashmir: Jehad or State *Sponsored Terrorism ?, Strategic Analysis,* 23(1), April 1999.

Kataria, Narain, *India's Nuclear Policy is Justified, Organiser,* 44(45), 24 May 1998.

Lt. Gen. Seth, K.M., Impact of Terrorism on India's Internal Security, *Man and Development,* 26(2), June 2004.

Malhotra, Inder, On Indo-Pakistan Negotiation of Kashmir, *Muslim India,* 15(173), May 1997.

Mayer, Frederick, W., Managing Domestic Differences in International Negotiations: The Strategic Use of Internal side Payments, *International Organization,* 46(4), Autumn 1992. (C) 1992 by the World Peace Foundation and the Massachusetts institute of Technology.

Mehta, Pratap Bhanu, India-Pakistan : The Enduring Stalemate, *Economic and Political Weekly,* 38(21), May 30, 2003.

Noorani, A.G., Disappearance in Kashmir, *Economic and Political Weekly,* 38(26), June 28, July 4, 2003.

Paranjape, Srikant, *India, Pakistan and Nuclear Test, (The Symbolism and Priorities), Mainstream,* 38(21), 13 May 2000.

Parthasarathy, Malini, An Elusive Peace with Pakistan, *Seminar* 509, January 2002.

Pawel, Milewski, Pakistan and India and the Events of September 11, *The Polish Quarterly of International Affairs,* 11(1), Winter 2002.

Puri, Balraj, A Post-Pokhran Policy For Kashmir, *Economic and Political Weekly,* 33(45), 7th November 1999.

Puri, Balraj, On Indo-Pakistan Relations, *Muslim India,* 15(180), December 1997.

Rajan, M.S., Nuclear Test: The Basic Issues, *Mainstream,* 36(37), 5 September 1998.

Raza Maroof, Pakistan Sponsored Insurgency in Kashmir : A Case Study, *Aakrosh,* 2(4), July 1999.

Sabur, Abdus, A.K.M., Indo-Pakistan Security, Relationship and the Kargil crisis , *biiss Journal*, 20(2), April 1999.

Sawhny, Karan K., Permanent Realities of India and Pakistan Relationship, *Mainstream*, 36(11), 7 March 1998.

Scindia, Madhavrao, Foreign Policy Approach, *Mainstream,* 39(42), October 6, 2001.

Seshia, Shaila, Divide and Rule in Indian Party Politics : The Rise of the Bharatiya Janata Party, *Asian Survey,* 38(11), November 1998.

Shahabuddin, Syed, An Approach to the Resolution of the Kashmir Dispute, *Mainstream,* 41(39), September 13, 2003.

Sikand, Yogindar, Changing Course of Kashmiri Struggle from National Liberation to Islamist Jihad ?, *Economic and Political Weekly,* 36(3), January 26, 2001.

Singh, Natwar K., NDA Foreign Policy or Directionless Drift, *Mainstream,* 38(33), August 5, 2000.

Zuberi, Matin, Pokhran II and Chagai, *World Focus,* 19(7-8), June-July 1998.

# Index

## I



## J



## K

**L**



**M**



**N**



**O**



**P**